SOUL COMPASS

TRUSTING YOUR INNER TRUTH TO NAVIGATE LIFE'S UNCERTAINTIES

CHERYL MARLENE

Soul Compass:
Trusting Your Inner Truth to Navigate Life's Uncertainties

© Copyright 2025 by Cheryl Marlene
All rights reserved.
No part of this book may be reproduced in any form or by any electronic or mechanical means, including information storage and retrieval systems, without written permission from the author, except for the use of brief quotations in a book review.

Published by
Soul Bright Press

Ebook ISBN: 978-1-945868-54-2
Paperback ISBN: 978-1-945868-52-8
Audio ISBN: 978-1-945868-59-7
Hardcover ISBN: 978-1-945868-53-5

Soul Compass Companion Journal
Paperback ISBN: 978-1-945868-55-9
Hardcover ISBN: 978-1-945868-57-3

CONTENTS

Don't Miss Anything!   v
Introduction   vii

1. What is Soul Compass?   1
2. Understanding Your Essential Self   9
3. The Journey Inward   21
4. Pathways of Presence   31
5. Living Within Inner Truth   42
6. Overcoming the Myth of Soul Purpose   57
7. The Primary Questions   65
8. Soul Calling: Hearing Your Inner Truth   73
9. Soul Paradox: The Key to Unlocking Fear   87
10. Soul Vision: Creating the Path   104
11. Life as a Spiral Path   125
12. Is this Where You Stop?   135

Ready to Learn More?   141
About Cheryl   143
Also by Cheryl Marlene   145

DON'T MISS ANYTHING!

Soul Compass Companion Journal, a companion journal with all the affirmations and questions suggested in this book, is available wherever you bought your copy of *Soul Compass*. Keep up-to-date with additional *Soul Compass* workbooks, workshops, and private sessions here:

https://www.cherylmarlene.com/soul-compass

Keep up with all of Cheryl's new books, workbooks, and workshops by subscribing to her newsletter, *SpiritualDeepDive.com*.

INTRODUCTION

*In this moment,
I choose my inner truth
to guide my life's path.*

Welcome to **Soul Compass**, a life process guiding you to follow the call of your soul, resolve life's inevitable paradox, and thrive within the empowerment of aligned vision.

I vividly remember a day I stood at a crossroads, overwhelmed and unsure of which path to take. The demands of the world were deafening, and I had no clear answers.

Behind me were all the turns of my life filled with both challenge and joy. Before me stretched many paths into the horizon, into the unknown.

Within these curves, I had learned to expect the unexpected. And because this wasn't the first crossroads, I felt it would not be my last life-changing challenge.

I took a deep breath. And I did something different from previous moments. Instead of grasping outward, I turned inward.

In the stillness within me, I heard a faint whisper of my inner truth. A voice that had always been there. Yet, by beginning inward, I heard its clarity reverberate within every cell of my body.

I took another deep breath and felt every layer of my body, mind, heart, and soul respond to this calling, its quiet strength filling my heart. In this truth, I knew *how* to continue. I felt the truth of my path. And like all journeys, I began – with one step.

The result of that one choice led me along a path of continual discovery and alignment, shaping the life process you now hold in your hands.

As you begin, please take a moment to pause creating your own stillness.

Close your eyes, place a hand over your heart, and ask yourself:

What truth is stirring within me right now?

Allow this question to anchor you as you step onto the spiral path before you, ready to explore the depths of your inner truth and its boundless possibilities.

Now, imagine you are a traveler, holding a compass which doesn't just point north but reveals the path of your heart, your soul, your fears, and your dreams. This compass doesn't promise a straight line. Instead, you are connected to possibility, so you won't lose your way.

The journey in this book will show you how to use this compass through the vast, spiraling path of self-discovery and alignment always at the crossroads of every moment of your life.

From my crossroad experiences, I think of this compass as my Soul Compass. And I have found that Soul Compass is a process of living life with inner truth. Soul Compass is also the guiding light within the depths of who you are and can become. Within Soul Compass, transformation and integration are not destinations but ways of being – an unfolding process of deepening awareness and growth, truth and expansion as your essential self.

At its heart, *Soul Compass* invites you to move beyond the rigid lines of destination-driven thinking and into the fluid, expansive motion of the spiral path. Maybe you have felt the pull of something greater, even if you couldn't name it. Perhaps, you have faced a choice so daunting it *seemed* impossible to move forward. This book is here to help you navigate these very moments, providing not purpose but a way of seeing the journey of life as sacred and transformative.

Life pushes you outward to find answers – to find truth anywhere but within. When this push happens, I have learned to focus on my compass within me. When I quit looking outward for the truth and for approval from others, when I learned to believe in myself, when I began to trust myself – this is when the needle of my inner truth revealed my foundation for new and shifted self-understanding.

In following this new foundation and learning to create my life from this self-understanding, I also learned to listen to the voice of truth within me. This is my inner truth and when I listen, I hear its whisper – its calling. Putting this inner truth into action I found I can envision my life. Doing so within inner truth means not only do calling and vision align, I find alignment within all of me, body, mind, heart, and soul.

And, yet, no matter what I do, the unknown exists. At first, I spent time trying to control, be perfect, anticipate the future – get out ahead so my destination always matched my vision – *always*. This is an exhausting and overwhelming way to live. Achievement can be had but at the expense of self, peace of mind, and balance within.

However, the unknown and the unexpected cannot be banished. Fear will pull and uncertainty will push. When I quit this fight and stopped the battle, I found an answer in obstacles – or that which *seems* to be an obstacle. I found that the transformation between the calling of truth and the execution of life vision is in the *seeming paradox* of the obstacle.

The key here is *seems* – where there *seems* to be an obstacle is exactly where you find the solution to resolve what *seems* to be the reason you cannot respond to calling or achieve vision.

Along the way, I learned that what resolved paradox and wove my calling together with my vision rested in the questions I asked. Simple questions – yet ones which did not shy from reality and truth. Questions which opened my heart and mind to unimagined possibility and new paths to satisfy calling and expand vision.

Questions, I found, are necessary to find direction and experience the depths of the journey. Questions unearth paradox and point toward resolution.

Plus, in the questions, I also found a path to unearth more layers of self-understanding. I found a positive personal process to release blocks as they arise and release the limitations to living within essential self. I opened the door to my ability to be fully present to myself and my life.

Finally, what seems to be the strangest paradox of all. I found that my Soul Compass did not lead to soul purpose or life purpose. Instead, I moved beyond the myth of these faux destinations and transformed the entire trajectory of my life's journey into the continual ebb and flow of calling, paradox, and vision.

Thus, I found the guidance of my soul compass within the challenges of my life, by turning lemons to margaritas, by listening to my heart and trusting myself to know my truth myself. This is me empowered – this is me claiming and living from my power within.

This book, **Soul Compass**, explains this process of living and describes the personal elements and questions needed to live with inner truth and vision.

Born from that moment when I stood at a crossroads in my own life, uncertain of which way to turn. **Soul Compass** is an illuminated map of possibility and power within.

This framework weaves together ancient wisdom and innovative perspectives, draws on my deep connection to the Akashic Records, and reflects my dedication to understanding how we, as human beings, navigate the complexities of modern life.

This journey does not promise quick fixes or one-size-fits-all solutions. Instead, find guidance toward practices of self-discovery empowering you to trust your inner truth and embrace your unique path. Life's challenges will not disappear, but your ability to navigate them will transform. With resilience, grace, and a sense of awe, you will discover how to move through life's spirals with greater ease and deeper personal trust.

Why Now?

We live in a world spinning with rapid change, uncertainty, and overwhelm – like a wheel turning too fast, its jarring motion vibrating through body, mind, heart, and soul. This overwhelm can feel like a tightening in your chest, a heaviness in your limbs, or a mind crowded with unrelenting noise, pulling you away from center.

In a culture prioritizing productivity over presence and external validation over inner trust, it is easy to lose sight of your own truth. *Soul Compass* challenges these paradigms, offering a radical invitation to live from the inside out. Imagine a compass, its needle steady amidst the chaos, guiding you back to your true north.

Soul Compass is a steadying force, inviting you to pause, breathe, and realign with your inner truth. Listen to your deepest calling, make space for your paradoxes, and envision a life rich, fulfilling, and aligned.

Whether reflecting on the past year, setting intentions for the future, or seeking guidance on a specific project, the Soul Compass process and its self-understanding foundation will help you value your personal truth while cultivating self-trust and self-awareness. You can transform fear into a catalyst for growth and develop a vision rooted in personal truth and possibility.

How to Use This Book

Soul Compass is structured to take you through a journey of personal exploration and integration. First, you will dive into an innovative foundation of self-understanding and power within without which the internal power of Soul Calling fades into the myths of yesterday. With this foundation unfolded, you explore the depth of calling, paradox, and vision to deeply understand and embody the guidance of your Soul Compass.

Each chapter begins and concludes with an affirmation expressing the energetic motion available within the concepts explored. Within each chapter you will find additional Soul Compass questions to help you tease out the stubborn, unhelpful habit, hidden fears, and sources of resistance and denial.

Questions serve to crack open the hardened shell and the protective measures which stand in the way of achieving the vision of your calling. These questions support the necessary thought work and heart work which opens the doors to clarity and deepest understanding. Soul Compass questions can be used in quiet moments for reflection and within intention in journaling, meditation, and personal Akashic Records inquiry.

Also I have created a companion journal where you may record response to each question. This journal includes all italicized questions and can be found where you bought this book. Also on my website, I have a special page for all things Soul Compass including specialized workshops and workbooks. Find this page here: https://www.cherylmarlene.com/soul-compass/

A Shared Journey

Soul Compass reflects the understanding that while we each walk our own unique paths, we are all interconnected in the grand tapestry of life.

As you integrate these practices into your life, remember individual alignment is not just a personal journey. Your presence with yourself inspires others in their journey inward. Like ripples spreading across a still pond, the insights you gain and the truth you embody influence your relationships, families, and communities.

Because we are all connected, when one person steps into alignment with their truth, this creates a resonance inspiring others to do the same, fostering a collective engagement to deeper meaning and shared connection.

This shared journey is reminder we are never truly alone. As you embark on your path, know you are connected to the whole. The spiral you walk is intersected by countless others seeking truth, meaning, and connection.

Together, we weave a tapestry of growth and alignment, where every step taken not only transforms life but also ripples outward to inspire and uplift others.

Every act of courage and resilience, every moment of alignment and integration, adds a thread to the fabric of collective growth and possibility. As you navigate the spiral path of your life, know your journey is part of a larger story, one connecting to greater harmony and deeper understanding.

As you engage with this book, please approach with curiosity and openness. The questions and processes within are not here to dictate how you should live but to empower you to uncover your truth and your choices. Trust the journey will unfold in alignment with truth, and know your willingness to explore is, in itself, a profound act of courage.

Your compass is in your hands and in your heart – let it guide you toward a life both expansive and connected, luminous and true.

Welcome to *Soul Compass*. Let's begin this transformative journey together.

With each turn of my path,

I embrace new possibility and

open to the luminous calling of my truth.

1

WHAT IS SOUL COMPASS?

In this moment,
I trust myself to navigate my life
with truth, discovery, and alignment.

WITHIN YOU IS A COMPASS GUIDING YOU THROUGH THE DYNAMIC currents of your journey. Not a structure for rigid paths or fixed endpoints, this Soul Compass is for navigating the uncertain waves of life with clarity, discovery, and alignment.

A Lighthouse for Inner Truth

In moments of chaos or obscurity, your compass light steadies you, its unwavering light offering reassurance and perspective. Whether you are navigating turbulent waters or the calm after the storm, your light reminds you of your direction, illuminating possibilities even when the horizon is shrouded in mist. You are invited to make choices rooted in personal truth and to embrace the ever-evolving spiral of your life's journey.

Soul Compass is a powerful approach to life and self-understanding with a set of questions to help you navigate life with confidence and clarity

At its heart, the navigational process of Soul Compass functions within three aspects of personal awareness:

Soul Calling:

This is the awareness of your inner truth. It's the voice within resonating with possibility, urging you toward the experiences, choices, and expressions aligned with your essential self. Soul Calling is not static, evolves as you do and reflects the dynamic interplay between your growth and the circumstances of your life. Living from this truth feels like stepping into warm sunlight or hearing the clear ring of a bell, a resonance awakening awareness deep within.

Soul Paradox:

This is the conflict arising when fears, beliefs, or assumptions *seem* to stand in opposition to your Soul Calling. Paradox is an invitation to explore and transcend these limitations. Imagine standing before a river, its currents rushing toward its destination but interrupted by jagged boulders. Soul Paradox is the bridge through that tension, where desire and doubt collide. By navigating the turbulence, you transform obstacles into pathways for growth.

Soul Vision:

This is the process of crafting a path to honor your calling while integrating the insights gained from navigating paradox. Soul Vision allows you to see and create possibilities aligned with your truth, even when the way forward is unclear. Picture it as a map drawn in golden ink, revealing paths as you take each step, inviting trust in both the known and the unknown.

Together, these interconnected elements form a comprehensive approach to self-discovery and alignment. They offer a way to live that is both deeply personal and profoundly connected to the transcendent currents of your life.

This navigation is empowered by the questions you ask yourself. Each aspect is opened by a primary question which will trigger more questions. The questions open the door to new possibility and supporting you to shift as needed to answer your call and achieve your vision. Questions are how you process paradox and overcome the obstacles of fear, overwhelm, and mistrust.

To answer your questions, you have thought work and heart work which take you into new layers of challenge and inquiry. Each new question raises new perspectives and new understanding with more personal work to examine, refine, release, and restore. This journey inward deepens how you understand yourself and, little by little, you move from calling, through paradox, and into vision.

A New Approach to Navigation

Traditional methods of navigating life often focus on rigid goals, linear progress, or externally defined purpose. These methods assume clarity comes from achieving a fixed destination or following a pre-set plan. Soul Compass challenges this paradigm, inviting you to step into a more fluid, intuitive approach.

Instead of striving to figure it all out before acting, Soul Compass encourages you to trust the process of unfolding. Like a flower blooming petal by petal or a river carving its way through a landscape, life's path reveals itself gradually, offering clarity in motion. Each moment of uncertainty becomes an invitation to listen inward, to realign with your truth, and to move forward through personal choice.

Remember, the path of life is not a straight line; rather a spiral randomly spinning with some turns to center quicker than others.

Other curves spin to the edge of the unknown and take time before returning with new understanding. As you experience your path's unique curves, you revisit familiar themes or step into new process, gaining new layers of understanding each time. Imagine your spiral as a dance – sometimes graceful, sometimes unpredictable – where each step, pivot, and pause deepens your connection to your inner truth. Soul Compass helps you embrace, this dance, this spiral path, using each twist and turn as an opportunity for growth and alignment.

This approach also emphasizes living from the inside out. This means you seek within your heart instead of deferring to the manipulation of truth from external authority. In a culture which values external validation over inner knowing, Soul Compass offers a radical shift.

You are invited to trust your truth first and trust this truth to inform your actions and decisions. By doing so, you create a life not only aligned with your essential self but also adaptable to life's inevitable changes and challenges. Inherently guided by inner personal truth, Soul Compass points out to you the direction of your spiral path in this moment, now.

The Elements in Action

To illustrate how Soul Compass works, imagine you are standing at a crossroads. The air feels heavy with possibility, a mix of excitement and trepidation swirling within. You feel a deep sense of longing to pursue a creative project and begin by asking yourself a question about your Soul Calling. Images, words, and a sense of direction will begin to bubble up.

Yet there are also doubts and fears emerging about whether you are good enough. You worry about failure and about choosing the *right* path. These fears form the core of your Soul Paradox, the place where your calling and your limitations *seem* to collide. They are the basis for you understanding the paradox or what *seems* to make calling impossible.

You explore the paradox, identifying and examining fears as they arise. Rather than letting these fears stop you, you use them as gateways for release and deeper understanding.

Finally, with this clarity, you craft a Soul Vision – a way forward honoring your calling while navigating the complexities of your paradox. Perhaps the vision is to begin small, carving out time for your project without overwhelming yourself. Or perhaps it's to seek support, inviting collaboration or mentorship to help you move forward. Or perhaps you know your next step on your own.

Unlimited in application, Soul Compass can be directed toward the broad arc of your awesome life or toward the process on a specific period of time like the new year, next month, or this week. You may also direct Soul Compass toward a project, a collaboration, or the conclusion of a cycle.

For example, imagine navigating a difficult relationship. You feel called to strengthen the bond, but past misunderstandings and lingering resentment create a sense of tension and doubt. Using Soul Compass, you begin by tuning into your Soul Calling – the desire for connection and harmony. This calling might evoke a sense of warmth and hope, reminding you why the relationship matters.

Next, you engage with the paradox, exploring the fears and emotions creating resistance and resentment. Perhaps you fell exposed or worry your efforts will not be reciprocated. By examining these fears, you gain clarity about your boundaries and needs.

Finally, you create a Soul Vision for moving forward – maybe it's initiating a heartfelt conversation, approaching the relationship with patience and empathy, or deciding to set healthy boundaries while maintaining compassion. This vision allows you to navigate the complexities of the relationship while staying true to your deeper values.

Another example begins by reflecting on the lessons of the past year as you prepare for the new one. You feel called to assess what has shaped you, but the enormity of the task feels overwhelming. Using Soul Compass, you start by connecting with your Soul Calling, identifying what truly resonated with your essential self over the past year – moments of growth, joy, or clarity. This calling might feel like a quiet pulse of gratitude or a spark of excitement for what's ahead.

Soul Compass can also be applied to crafting the path of a new project whether personal or professional. And within these journeys there are supporting callings which join together to achieve the primary calling of the broad vision.

Next, you explore the paradox: fears of letting go of old patterns or the discomfort of embracing new possibilities. By delving into these fears, you begin to see how they've shaped your experiences and where they've held you back.

With this insight, you craft a Soul Vision for the new year – guidance integrating the lessons you've learned and setting intentions aligned with your truth. Perhaps your vision includes dedicating more time to creativity, deepening relationships, or stepping boldly into an opportunity you've long considered. This process transforms reflection into purposeful action, setting the stage for a year of truth and growth.

Beyond the Destination

One of the most transformative aspects of Soul Compass is its emphasis on process over destination. In a world equating success with achieving specific outcomes, this approach can feel both odd and liberating. Soul Compass reminds you that the *journey* itself is where growth, alignment, and fulfillment occur.

This doesn't mean goals and outcomes have no place. They do, but they are not the ultimate measure of success. Instead, success is redefined and experienced in each moment of your journey. This move away from destination-thinking shifts to the elements of your vision. Your spiral path is found in your ability to stay connected to your truth, to navigate challenges with courage and grace, and to continuously refine your vision as you learn and grow. Your compass steers by the stars in a process of dynamic navigation relying on trust and adaptation rather than rigid precision.

Soul Compass is not about finding the one perfect answer or solution. It's about cultivating the tools and practices allowing you to respond to life's questions in the moment with intention and integrity. You learn to trust yourself even when the way forward is unclear. You realize you have within you the wisdom and resilience to navigate whatever arises.

To hear and follow your truth within, Soul Compass requires that you learn to be present to yourself. This process asks you to define and connect with your essential self. To focus on your inward journey without these fundamentals of self-understanding and without the willingness to be responsible for your life, there will be no forward motion. Instead, you leave yourself dependent on outside motions, alien to your personal truth and power within.

An Invitation to Begin

As you step into this journey, picture a path bathed in warm light, each step revealing more of your truth, each choice bringing to you what you need with grace and ease. The air is alive with possibility, and every step within your spiral feels like a reclamation of your truth. Remember Soul Compass is not something you do perfectly. This is a practice – a lifelong companion, evolving as you evolve, guiding you through the spiral of your life's unfolding.

Now with a sense of the process, you begin this journey by exploring your essential self and seeking your journey inward. Next is to consider personal presence, the pathways of personal discovery, and how to live within inner truth. These form the foundation of Soul Compass, enhance your journey, and imbue life with truth, clarity, and direction.

Next is consideration of the primary questions of Soul Compass and then a deep dive into the three aspects of the Soul Compass so that you can make this process your own.

Thus, as you move forward, you will delve deeper into each element of Soul Compass, exploring how to attune to your calling, work through your paradoxes, and create a vision aligned with your truth. This is your invitation to navigate life with clarity, courage, and your power within. Trust you are exactly where you need to be and let your Soul Compass guide you forward.

In this moment,

I am exactly where I need to be.

2

UNDERSTANDING YOUR ESSENTIAL SELF

In this moment,
I am open to discovering
the depths of my inner being.

Who am I?

When you scrape away the layers, and get to your center – who are you?

At center is your essential self. Not a fixed idea or an external standard. Instead, find the ever-present motion of you, drawing together all aspects of your being: body, mind, heart, and soul.

Within essential self, life experience intersects with your unique divine nature, creating a focal point of clarity, authenticity, and truth. Here is the pulse of life guiding you to learn, grow, and love.

Your essential self is not a mask you wear or a role you play. It is not defined by the pain or challenges you have endured. Instead, it is the pure essence shining through when the layers of life's camouflage – trauma, disappointment, outdated beliefs – are cleared away. This is the self you seek, the self seeking you, the self holding your clearest awareness of inner truth.

To engage deeply with the Soul Compass approach – whether it is understanding your soul calling, navigating soul paradox, or envisioning your soul's path – you begin here, with your essential self.

Thus, essential self is both foundation and guide which relies primarily on four essential qualities: trust, integrity, courage, and resiliency. Each ignite truth and together empower you to embrace your life with confidence and clarity.

Alive with the rhythm of your being and becoming , your essential self is not static. Hear its inner voice urging you to learn, to grow, to love, and to discover. By aligning with the deep personal awareness of your essential self, you open the door to profound transformation, empowered integration, and the harmony of personal alignment. From this place of balance and unity, you are prepared to move forward, ready to listen to the whispers of your soul, and chart a course which honors your truth.

Connection with Inner Truth

Your essential self is the seat of your inner truth. Not merely an aspect of who you are, essential self is the entirety of your being, the source from which your deepest truths arise. Inner truth is not something external to be discovered. Inner truth is something intrinsic to be remembered, a resonance aligned with your essential self when you are present and attuned to your whole being.

At its heart, the essential self is the intersection of body, mind, heart, and soul, where clarity and authenticity naturally emerge. This intersection creates a dynamic presence constantly evolving, reflecting the ever-changing yet always authentic nature of inner truth. Just as the essential self is not static, inner truth is also alive, shaped by your experiences, growth, and evolving awareness.

The relationship between the essential self and inner truth is symbiotic. The essential self provides the clarity and foundation for recognizing inner truth, while inner truth, in turn, anchors you in your essential self. Together, they form the compass guiding your journey, offering steadiness even in the face of uncertainty.

Clearing the Debris

Life's journey gathers behind layers of debris – pain, sorrow, trauma, and disappointment – which obscure your essential self. Like a veil, these layers cloud your ability to see and feel the vibrant essence at your core. Yet, the essential self remains steadfast, waiting for you to rediscover its light, to feel its illumination, to know you shine from within.

Clearing the debris is not about erasing the past or denying its impact. Instead, it is about peeling back the layers that no longer define you, releasing what has weighed you down, and allowing your true essence to radiate. This process can be challenging, requiring honesty, courage, and self-compassion. Yet, this is also deeply liberating, reconnecting you with yourself, your wholeness, unbroken and naturally resilient.

When you align with your essential self, you begin to see yourself not as a collection of fragmented experiences but as a unified, dynamic being. This alignment empowers you to live authentically, connected to your truth and guided by the motion of your becoming.

Navigating with your Soul Compass depends upon understanding and connecting with your essential self. Both starting point and completion, essential self ignites your journey and is the point of return for each motion of calling, paradox, and vision.

Intersection and Integration

Your essential self exists at the intersection of all that makes you uniquely you. Where your life experiences meet your divine nature, the threads of your body, mind, heart, and soul are woven together into a tapestry of wholeness. This integration is not a singular moment of arrival; it is an ongoing process of balance and unity.

Think of your essential self as the connective point where all layers of your being converge. This, your center, embraces your physical presence, intellectual insights, emotional depth, and spiritual awareness. In this integration, you find not only a sense of who you are but also the clarity to discern your inner truth. It is here, in this convergence, you access the profound wisdom and presence which guide your life.

Your essential self is a place of perpetual motion and alignment with the ebb and flow of life. Your essential self is at the center of this cyclical journey where every experience, every moment of growth, and every lesson learned leads you back to the center of who you are.

With each turn of the spiral path, you return to your essential self, now at a deeper level of understanding and alignment. Like the changing seasons, the essential self reflects the cycles of life – renewing, releasing, and growing with each step and each return.

Within this dynamic motion, the essential self is never static nor confined. Alive, evolving, the journey of essential self always brings you back to alignment with your inner truth and your power within.

Embodying the Essential Self

Understanding your essential self is not enough; your journey requires embodiment. To embody your essential self is to live in alignment with the core of who you are, bringing balance and unity to your body, mind, heart, and soul. This embodiment becomes the compass guiding your choices, actions, and relationships as you engage deeply with the Soul Compass approach.

Your essential self thrives when all aspects of your being work in harmony. This unity is not about perfection; it is about balance and integration. Each part – body, mind, heart, and soul – plays a vital role in supporting the whole.

Body: The body is your foundation, the vessel through which your essential self expresses itself in the physical world. When you listen to your body's wisdom, you create a connected and stable connection to your inner truth. Ask: *In this moment, how does my body feel?*

Mind: Your mind processes, analyzes, and reflects, offering clarity and insight. When aligned with your essential self, the mind becomes a tool for understanding and is able to move beyond fear and self-doubt. Ask: *In this moment, what thoughts are filling my mind?*

Heart: The heart is the seat of emotion, connection, and compassion. Bridging the rational mind and the intuitive soul, your heart helps you navigate life with empathy and love. Ask: *In this moment, what emotions are present in my heart?*

Soul: The soul is the eternal aspect of your being, the thread connecting you to the divine and the transcendent. Your soul offers the expansive vision that grounds your essential self in the larger tapestry of existence and experience. Ask: *In this moment, what insights is my soul offering?*

Fundamental Qualities of Essential Self

In embracing and embodying your essential self, four fundamental personal qualities help you navigate your life through inner truth. Trust, integrity, courage, and resiliency serve as the foundation for your journey, supporting you as you align with your inner truth, navigate the deeper aspects of your Soul Compass, and maintain connection with essential self.

Trust

Trust is the cornerstone of your relationship with your essential self. Trust is the quiet confidence that your inner truth will guide you, even when the path ahead is uncertain. Trust allows you to step into the unknown, knowing your essential self is always present, steady, and reliable.

Self-trust is particularly vital in this process. External voices, societal expectations, or past disappointments may cause you to doubt your inner knowing. Cultivating trust means tuning into your own inner truth and recognizing it as the compass pointing you toward awareness and alignment.

Consider a moment when you trusted your instincts and found a meaningful outcome. Ask:

How do I feel when I rely on my inner truth?

In daily life, how can I strengthen trust?

Within Soul Compass and as you explore Soul Calling, trust allows you to distinguish between external expectations and what truly resonates with your inner truth. Trust in your essential self ensures you follow what feels aligned, even if the path is unconventional.

Integrity

Integrity is your ability to do what you promise and is reflected in the alignment of your actions, values, and truth. Living in harmony with your essential self, integrity ensures what you do and how you show up in the world reveals who you truly are. Integrity is not about perfection; it is about authenticity and a willingness to hold yourself accountable to your own truth.

When you act with integrity, you honor the balance of your body, mind, heart, and soul. You create a life resonating with your essential self, fostering a sense of wholeness and clarity. Integrity also provides a steadying force in moments of challenge, helping you remain grounded in your values and calling.

Lean into integrity by identifying where in your life you feel out of alignment with your essential self.

What small change can I make today to bring greater integrity into my life?

How can I hold myself accountable to my inner truth?

Navigating Soul Paradox requires integrity – the ability to hold contradiction while remaining aligned with your essential self. Integrity provides a steady anchor in the face of uncertainty or contradiction.

Courage

Courage is the willingness to step into vulnerability, uncertainty, and transformation. Courage is needed to face the layers of debris hiding your essential self and to embrace the dynamic motion of becoming. Courage is not the absence of fear; it is the determination to move forward despite fear.

Your essential self thrives when you are courageous enough to challenge outdated beliefs, explore new possibilities, and let go of what no longer serves you. Each act of courage deepens your connection to your inner truth, allowing your essential self to shine more brightly.

Reflect on a fear or hesitation that has been holding you back. Ask:

What is one small, courageous step I can take today to face fear or hesitation?

How can I find courage to face fear?

To envision and pursue a bold Soul Vision, courage is essential. It empowers you to take risks, embrace transformation, and align your actions with your deeper truth even when the outcome is uncertain.

Resiliency

Resiliency is the ability to adapt and grow through life's challenges. This is the quality that allows you to bend without breaking, to learn from difficulty, and to emerge stronger and more aligned with your essential self.

Resiliency is not about suppressing pain or denying struggle. Resiliency is about acknowledging life's challenges and finding ways to move through them with grace and strength. Your essential self is the origin of your resiliency, offering the clarity and balance needed to navigate both the highs and lows of your journey. To become more resilient, begin by releasing self-judgment. Ask yourself:

How can I become more adaptable within the challenges of life?

How can I learn from life's difficulties?

Why do I push myself to be perfect?

The journey through the Soul Compass framework is not always smooth. A resilient foundation ensures you can adapt, grow, and remain connected to your essential self, even in the face of setbacks or challenges.

Overall, when faced with a challenge, take a moment to center yourself. To find a path forward honoring your truth, ask:

What is my essential self showing me in this moment?

These four qualities – trust, integrity, courage, and resiliency – are not separate from your essential self. They represent the expression of your essential self. As you cultivate and embody these qualities, you create a solid foundation for your Soul Compass, empowering yourself to engage deeply with your calling, paradox, and vision. Let these qualities guide you as you explore the vast potential of your essential self.

Essential Self within Your Soul Compass

Remember your Soul Compass process consists of three elements: Soul Calling, Soul Paradox, and Soul Vision. At the heart of each is your essential self, guiding and aligning you with your inner truth. By connecting with your essential self, you can navigate each aspect with clarity, authenticity, and confidence.

Your essential self is in the quiet voice helping you discern what resonates deeply. Acting as a filter, essential self sifts through external noise and societal expectations to reveal the calling aligned with your truth. This connection allows you to identify what truly matters to you and what direction feels most authentic. For example, tap into your essential self's perspective on calling with this question:

What is my essential self guiding me to explore or create?

Take time to sit with this question. Trust the answers which emerge from within, even if they feel unexpected or unconventional. Your essential self knows what resonates most deeply with your body, mind, heart, and soul.

Life is full of paradox – moments when clarity and mystery coexist. Your essential self provides the steadiness to hold both, offering a sense of balance in midst of *seeming* contradiction. It reminds you truth exists in layers, and understanding often emerges through embracing opposition. To explore and move beyond, try this question:

How can I use the steadiness of my essential self to navigate contradictions?

Reflect on a situation in your life that feels paradoxical. Allow your essential self to guide acceptance of complexity to find clarity within.

To envision and pursue a bold Soul Vision requires both courage and clarity. Your essential self fuels this vision, providing the inspiration to imagine what is possible and the courage to act even in the face of uncertainty and the unknown. By staying rooted in your essential self, you align your vision with your deepest truth creating a path both intentional and authentic. Explore possibilities by asking:

Living fully aligned with my essential self, what will my life look like?

Spend time visualizing this alignment. Within this, think on the choices, actions, or dreams which feel most true to you. Feel your presence and how trust, integrity, courage, and resiliency are woven together into an integrated tapestry of balance and clarity. Then feel into how you can bring this vision into your daily life.

By tying the essential self to these elements of Soul Compass, and contemplating reflective questions for each, you empower yourself to engage with your compass process in a deeply personal and transformative way. This integration shows how the essential self is not just a guide but the very foundation fueling your journey.

Once embodied, your essential self becomes the energy and the fuel of your compass, illuminating life's complexities with clarity and authenticity. Circulating within, essential self's motion brings awareness to the elements of your Soul Compass.

Your essential self is not separate from these aspects of the Soul Compass approach. Rather, essential self along with inner truth and personal presence is the foundation and the touchstone for each step of your journey.

The essential self brings motion to the compass needle in your journey. Just as a compass needle consistently points north, your essential self always orients you toward inner truth. This needle is steady, even when the map of life is unclear or shifting. No matter how tumultuous external circumstances may become, your essential self offers the clarity and connection needed to navigate with confidence and authenticity.

When challenges appear, and the path *seems* blocked, return to your awareness of essential self. Within its steady guidance, you will be reminded of what is true and aligned with your deepest essence. It may not always provide immediate answers, but it will always point you toward the next step, anchoring you in your journey.

Empowering Your Essential Self

Your essential self is the heart of who you are, the dynamic and evolving core integrating every aspect of your being – body, mind, heart, and soul. At the intersection of your life's experiences is this your unique divine essence, offering clarity, authenticity, and truth as you navigate your journey.

Embodying your essential self is not a one-time achievement; it is a lifelong practice of presence, alignment, and growth. By understanding and embodying your essential self, you create a foundation to support every aspect of your Soul Compass. From this place of alignment, you can explore your Soul Calling with confidence, embrace Soul Paradox with grace, and envision your soul's path with clarity and purpose.

Trust, integrity, courage, and resiliency are the pillars to strengthen and support this connection, empowering you to face challenges, release outdated beliefs, and move forward with a sense of balance and unity. These qualities are not just tools – they are reflections of your essential self in motion, guiding you toward a life of awareness, transformation, integration, and alignment.

This is not a journey of perfection or destination. This is a continual process of being and becoming. Each moment invites you to connect more deeply with your essential self, to peel back the debris hiding your truth, and to step boldly into the rhythm of your being.

As you move into the next steps of your Soul Compass journey, carry with you this understanding: your essential self is always present, always guiding you. Your essential self is your anchor, your guide, and your inspiration as you explore the profound depths of your life's journey. Within this inner guidance, you can trust yourself to muster the courage to face your journey with integrity, resiliency, and deepest inner truth.

In this moment,

I embrace the harmony of

my body, mind, heart, and soul

as my essential self.

3

THE JOURNEY INWARD

In this moment,
I step into my stillness and inner truth.

FEEL YOURSELF STANDING AT THE EDGE OF A QUIET ROOM LIT BY SOFT light. The air carries a faint warmth, and the light casts long, soft shadows holding quiet promise. The hum of the outside world fades into a distant murmur, leaving only the steady rhythm of your breath and the gentle rustle of fabric as you settle into stillness. The hum of the outside world fades, leaving the creative rhythm of your breath and the steady beat of your heart.

This is the moment where your journey inward begins – an intentional turning away from the noise of external demands to the sanctuary within. The moment you begin to listen inward can feel both freeing and disorienting, like stepping into a quiet room after a storm. There's a pause – a breath – before the clarity of your own voice begins to emerge. Not just the retreat of demand – this is a moment of reclamation of your truth and your trust in you.

In this moment, step into this space of stillness knowing you can cultivate self-trust and embrace the integrated dynamics of body, mind, heart, and soul. Without this inner embrace, the guidance offered by Soul Compass remains distant, like a voice carried on the wind but never quite reaching your ears. The journey inward is not merely an initial step. This is a lifelong dance with your essential self as you learn to live from the inside out.

From External to Internal

If this inner journey feels uncomfortable or, maybe, impossible, may your experience in reading this book help soften your walls of resistance. May you learn to receive and believe in your inner truth.

Many of the controlling external efforts around you want to invalidate your personal voice of truth. Plus, you may also be aware of your critical voice – that snarky judgmental, inner voice which sneers at every thought, every feeling, every choice you dare make on your own. To hear inner truth requires you learn to quiet the critical voice and open your heart to hear and receive personal truth as Soul Calling.

Modern culture often feels like a storm of expectations, pulling you in countless directions at once. The weight of societal standards, the lure of external achievements, and the chatter of others' opinions create a whirlwind drowning out your inner voice of truth. As though you've been handed a map drawn by strangers, each line and symbol reflecting someone else's idea of where you should go, what you should do, and who you should be.

However, the inward journey invites you to set this map aside. Rather, you are asked to close your eyes and listen to the compass of your own soul – that steady, quiet pull toward what feels true to you. Take a moment to reflect:

What external expectations have shaped my decisions recently?

What might shift if I pause to honor my inner voice first?

What shifts when I honor myself by believing I can find the steps of my journey?

Let these questions guide you as you begin to listen inward. This doesn't mean ignoring the world around you. Instead create a sacred pause to honor your voice before taking external factors into account. This inward alignment lays the foundation for connecting with your Soul Calling, navigating the complexities of your Soul Paradox, and crafting a Soul Vision aligned with your deepest truths.

Living from the inside out requires trust in your inner compass. This trust is not about certainty or having all the answers. This trust is about believing in your ability to navigate the unknown with intention. Trust feels like the warmth of a fire on a cold night or the grounding weight of your feet pressing into the earth. It's a quiet strength, the knowledge that you can face life's complexities with openness and courage.

When you choose to trust yourself, you create fertile ground for growth, connection, and alignment – qualities essential for embracing your Soul Compass.

Integration of Body, Mind, Heart, and Soul

The journey inward is not a single path but a weaving together of the four essential facets of your essential self. Imagine these elements as the strings of a harp, each contributing to the harmony of your life's melody. When one string is neglected or out of tune, the song becomes discordant. True alignment requires the integration of these facets into a cohesive, integrated whole.

Body:

Your body is the vessel through which you experience life. Holding profound wisdom your physical form speaks to you through sensations, instincts, and rhythms. Imagine your body as a sturdy tree, its roots anchoring you to the present moment and its branches and leaves gathering nurturance and support. Honoring its signals – whether it's the need for rest, movement, or nourishment – grounds your choices in reality and helps you move with intention. Place your hand on your chest. Feel the rise and fall of your breath.

What is my body asking for in this moment?

Mind:

Like a compass needle, your mind offers direction through analysis and reflection. It articulates your desires and helps you navigate practical challenges. When aligned with the other facets, the mind becomes a trusted ally, offering clarity without the noise of overthinking. Picture your mind as a clear sky after a storm, expansive and full of possibility.

Recall a recent decision you've made.

How do my thoughts support or hinder my clarity?

Heart:

Your heart is the seat of emotion, connection, and vulnerability. Your heart is where compassion and passion meet, creating a space for deep relationships and authentic choices. Imagine your heart as a flame, steady and warm, illuminating the path of your connections with yourself and others. Think of a moment when you felt deeply connected to someone or something.

What does my heart reveal about my life experience?

Soul:

The soul is the essence of who you are beyond the material world. It connects you to the infinite, to something greater than yourself. Your soul feels like the vastness of a starlit sky, reminding you of your place in the universe and your potential to dream without limits. Imagine the night sky.

What does my soul feel drawn to in the sky's infinite vastness?

When these facets of self work together, you cultivate a sense of wholeness empowering you to navigate life's uncertainties with resilience and confidence. This integration supports the broader framework of Soul Compass, ensuring your inner alignment fuels the clarity needed to engage, navigate, and bring your vision to life.

This journey inward also mirrors the cycles of nature, where balance and renewal emerge through the ebb and flow of seasons. Just as the tides rise and fall and the trees shed their leaves to grow anew, your inward alignment adapts to the rhythms of your life, offering connection and renewal. Each element brings its own wisdom, and together they form the foundation of your inner alignment. But when one facet is neglected – when the body is ignored, the mind races unchecked, the heart is closed off, or the soul is forgotten – imbalance occurs, making it harder to access the full guidance of Soul Compass.

This integration of your body, mind, heart, and soul creates a foundation for trust. By uniting these facets, you begin to understand that alignment is not an abstract ideal but a lived experience, rooted in everyday moments. When these elements are harmonized, you cultivate a profound sense of self-awareness and self-belief, making trust a natural extension of your inner balance.

Trust as a Practice

Building trust in yourself is like planting a garden. It requires patience, care, and the willingness to return to it, even when weeds appear, or storms pass through. Self-trust is not a one-time decision; it grows through consistent engagement. Each time you listen to your inner voice and act in alignment with it, you strengthen the roots of that trust.

Like the cycles of the moon or the changing of the seasons trust is not static. Trust ebbs and flows. Some days, trust in yourself may shine brightly, clear and unwavering like a full moon. Other times, it may feel hidden, like the new moon waiting for its light to return. This cyclical nature isn't a flaw – it's a reminder that trust grows through practice, intention, and renewal.

There is a direct connection between quieting or ignoring your critical voice and trusting yourself and your voice of truth. In some respects, building trust is more vanquishing limiting self-judgment and the knee-jerk criticism which rolls off the tongue with ease. As your critical voice takes a back seat to your deeper inner voice, trust steps forward and claims its position as guide to the essential self's intrinsic truth. Jettisoning the lead position of your critical voice opens the door for trust and truth to step forward as the rightful guide of your spiral path.

To support the strengthening of self-trust there are many possible paths. Essentially, create space to hear your inner voice without external commentary. Try quiet reflection or meditation where you spend a few minutes each day focusing on your breath, repeating an affirmation or contemplating a question.

Intentionally, find moments where you pause and connect to your inner compass. Daily rituals are particularly helpful here. Create a set of affirmations to say first thing in the morning or journal each evening using the same prompt or question. Repetition can soften the edges of protection and habits of denial.

Affirmations are particularly beneficial in reinforcing self-trust and courage. The affirmation describes your path of transformation and reinforces the current cycle of integration. Take a judgment of your critical voice and flip the meaning into an affirming direction.

Here are several examples where the negative is shifted to positive and supportive:

I am never aware of the right things becomes *I trust my inner wisdom to guide me.*

I always make stupid mistakes becomes *Each step I take is in alignment with my truth.*

I always miss opportunity becomes *Everything I need moves towards me quickly, easily, and safely.*

Trust can also be deepened by letting go of self-judgment. Acknowledge and release critical thoughts that arise when you make mistakes. Instead, frame these moments as opportunities to learn and grow. Practicing forgiveness toward yourself strengthens your ability to move forward with confidence.

Imagine carrying a heavy backpack filled with stones, each one labeled with a past mistake or regret. With every step, the weight slows you down, making the journey harder than necessary. Letting go of self-judgment is like setting that backpack down. At first, it feels unfamiliar, but as you take the next steps, your body feels lighter, your breath comes easier, and you realize just how much the burden was holding you back. Embracing this practice allows you to move forward with grace and self-compassion, ready to navigate new challenges with trust.

Remember, trust is not about getting everything right. Like tending a garden, there will be seasons of growth and seasons of rest. Mistakes will happen, but they are not failures. They are invitations to learn, to adjust, and to keep showing up for yourself with compassion. Trust thrives in an environment where perfectionism is replaced with patience, where each small step is celebrated as part of the journey. This practice of trust empowers you to fully engage with the Soul Compass framework, building the resilience needed to trust your voice of truth.

The Courage to Look Within

The journey inward is not for the faint of heart. This motion asks you to face fears, insecurities, and wounds buried for years. Imagine peeling back layers of armor, each revealing a softer, more truthful part of yourself. This process is both vulnerable and empowering. This is the act of reclaiming the silenced or forgotten parts of your essential self.

Courage is needed to follow your life's path. Courage when moments of growth are followed by stillness. When choice is followed by delay or a seemingly downward turn. Courage is required to steady your boat and retrieve yourself when life *seems* to capsize. Just as a field lies fallow in winter to prepare for spring's renewal, moments of quiet reflection lay the groundwork for courage to flourish. Trust these cycles. Every phase has intention.

Courage also means stepping away from the distractions pulling you outward. Think of the stillness of a forest after a fresh snowfall, where the quiet feels both vast and intimate, inviting you to reconnect with the deep essence of who you are. In the same way, the journey inward offers a natural rhythm of pause and reflection, grounding you like the roots of a tree deep in the earth.

In a world filled with constant noise – phones buzzing, schedules overflowing – choosing stillness becomes an act of defiance and empowerment. Think of a calm lake, the surface reflecting the sky's vastness. Here is the courage to be still, to listen, and to honor whatever arises from within.

An Invitation to Begin

As you close this chapter, take a moment for reflection. Write down one area of your life where you want to listen inward more deeply. Ask:

What small action can I take today to honor my inward intention?

Let this be a first step toward strengthening your connection with your inner truth.

As you embark on this inward journey, know you are not alone. Within a circle of travelers, each carries their own compass, and each seeks their own truth. The path may look different for everyone, but the intention is shared: to rediscover and trust the truth within.

Close your eyes and take a deep breath. Feel the rhythm of your body, the quiet hum of your mind, the steady beat of your heart, and the infinite expanse of your soul. Here are your guides. Listen to the whispers of your truth and trust that within you lies the wisdom to navigate whatever life brings.

This is the foundation of Soul Compass: a deep, unshakable connection to your inner truth, empowering you to embrace the unknown with trust and courage. Let this journey inward be the light guiding you forward, one step closer to living in alignment with your truth. You are on a path illuminated by the soft glow of starlight, each step bringing you closer to the quiet strength and wisdom within. This is your journey inward – a transformative path where every choice reveals more of who you truly are.

Know in your heart, this journey is yours to shape. The questions and reflections included here are guideposts. The path you walk will always be uniquely your own. Trust in your capacity to navigate this path with courage and trust. Know the answers you seek already exist within you.

In this moment,

I trust my inner truth to guide me.

4

PATHWAYS OF PRESENCE

**In this moment,
I am present to the entirety of me.**

To journey with your Soul Compass is to first anchor yourself in the presence of your essential self. This state of personal awareness is the necessary foundation from which you will explore calling, paradox, and vision.

Your essential self is like the still point at the center of a spinning wheel – stable and unchanging even as life's circumstances swirl around it.

When you are present to the nature of your essential self, you enter a state of clarity, balance, and authenticity. Unfolding from center are the four pathways of presence, power, and growth. Present to your amazing self you step into: awareness, transformation, integration, and alignment.

Awareness of your inner truth works hand in hand with presence. Being present allows you to step beyond distractions and external influences, creating a clear space where your inner truth can emerge.

This truth – your essential self – acts as a guide, helping you discern what aligns with your principles and intentions and what does not. In moments of presence, you become attuned to the subtle signals of your inner world: the quiet knowing directing your choices, the sense of ease when you are aligned, and the discomfort when you stray from your path. This dynamic foundation enables authentic and intentional navigation of life.

Thus, personal presence is not static but dynamic, a living connection to your truth in each moment. Presence is the foundation of your journey, the point of return when you seek clarity or renewal. Soul Compass functions within presence, guiding you to discover and embody your Soul Calling, reconcile your Soul Paradox, and illuminate your Soul Vision.

Presence is the necessary element in your four growth pathways of your Soul Compass. Each pathway requires that you be present to yourself and your life experience. Plus, your essential self plays a unique role in each of the four pathways:

These four pathways of the Soul Compass are deeply interconnected, creating a continuous cycle of growth and self-discovery. Each pathway supports and reinforces the others, ensuring that your journey is connected to your essential self.

In Awareness, the essential self acts as a mirror, reflecting the truth of who you are and enabling you to see beyond distractions or self-imposed limitations. In awareness, you know you and through this knowing choose, experience, and live life.

By cultivating awareness, you develop clarity about the patterns, beliefs, and truths shaping your life. This clarity lays the groundwork for transformation, allowing you to identify what needs to shift and where growth can occur.

In Transformation, essential self serves as a steady anchor, providing stability as you navigate the discomfort and uncertainty growth often brings.

Plus, transformation deepens integration. As you embrace change and release limitations, you gain new insights and lessons. These are then woven into your life through the process of integration, ensuring that your growth is sustainable and meaningful.

In Integration, the essential self weaves together disparate parts of your experience, creating a cohesive and harmonious awareness of self.

By integrating your experiences, you create a cohesive understanding of yourself that naturally guides your choices. This strengthens alignment, allowing your actions to reflect your inner truth more authentically.

In Alignment, essential self acts as a compass, consistently pointing you toward choices and actions resonating with your deepest truth, revealing your balance and harmony.

Finally, alignment fuels further awareness. Living in alignment with your truth and vision enhances your awareness, as you become more attuned to the present moment and the evolving aspects of your journey.

Together, these pathways create a dynamic process that is both cyclical and life-supporting. Let's explore more for each pathway.

Awareness: The Starting Point

Awareness begins here, now with the present moment. Like stepping into a clearing in a dense forest, awareness is an inner space where the noise of the world fades, and you can clearly see the path ahead. When you are fully present, you connect to the clarity and truth of your essential self. Awareness is the foundation from which all other pathways flow, as it invites you to observe, reflect, and understand the deeper truths of your life.

There are many ways to cultivate and deepen your awareness. For example, to anchor awareness in the present moment, spend time noticing the details of your environment and your internal state without judgment. Notice feelings of connection, resistance, denial, or peace. Notice how both action and thought influence awareness. Explore questions such as:

> *What emotions or thoughts arise most frequently for me?*

> *What am I currently avoiding deserving of my attention?*

To help distinguish between your essential self and your inner actions, imagine yourself standing at the edge of a tranquil river. Picture your thoughts and feelings flowing gently downstream, leaving you connected to the stillness of your essential self. This is you being aware of you.

Use questions to tap into your awareness:

> *What patterns have I noticed in my thoughts and behaviors recently?*

> *How do I currently feel connected to my essential self?*

> *What truths have emerged as I've become more aware of my inner world?*

Consider Sarah, who found herself overwhelmed by a demanding job and personal obligations. She began a daily mindfulness practice, dedicating just ten minutes each morning to observe her thoughts without judgment. Over time, she noticed a recurring theme of self-doubt that was affecting her decisions. By reflecting on this pattern, Sarah uncovered the roots in past experiences and gained the clarity to start addressing both the pattern and its source . This newfound awareness allowed her to set boundaries and prioritize her well-being, fostering a deeper connection to her essential self.

Transformation: The Path of Growth

Transformation is the process of growth and change which arises from embracing your truth. Akin to a caterpillar becoming a butterfly, sometimes transformation is uncomfortable yet ultimately a liberating journey. Transformation involves releasing limiting beliefs, healing wounds, and stepping into a more expansive understanding of yourself. Transformation requires courage, vulnerability, and trust in the unfolding of your journey.

To initiate transformation, identify limiting beliefs and reflect on patterns or fears holding you back. Use your awareness and imagine walking through a door separating your current self from the person you wish to become. Envision shedding layers of doubt as you step forward. Become aware of the differences to identify what stays and what is released.

Use these questions to reflect on transformation:

What belief is keeping me from stepping into my potential?

What limiting belief have I released recently, and how has it shifted my perspective?

How have I embraced vulnerability in my journey?

What transformations am I currently experiencing, and what do they teach me about my essential self?

For example, Tom struggled with a fear of public speaking, limiting his professional growth. After identifying this fear as rooted in a childhood experience of being ridiculed, he decided to confront it through a series of small, intentional steps. He joined a local speaking group and practiced sharing brief stories in a supportive environment. Each time he embraced vulnerability, his confidence grew. Over time, Tom transformed his fear into a source of strength, allowing him to confidently take on leadership roles.

Integration: Embodying Wholeness

Integration is the act of bringing together the lessons, insights, and growth of your journey into a cohesive whole. Imagine weaving a tapestry, where each thread – light and dark – contributes to the beauty and strength of the design. It is about acknowledging every part of your experience – the light and the shadow – and recognizing their essential role in your wholeness.

Integration works intentionally to settle the shifts of transformation into everyday life. For example, write about the connections between your past experiences and your present self. Ask:

What lessons have I carried forward, and how do they serve me now?

Bring awareness of your integration through ritual or a new tradition. Create a small piece of art – a sketch, poem, or melody – that represents your journey and growth. Create a new affirmation which helps you embody your new shifts. Begin or end each day listing three moments or insights you're grateful for and how they integrate into your life.

In reflection, ask:

How do my past experiences continue to shape my current path?

What lessons have I fully integrated into my daily life?

In what ways do I honor both the light and shadow aspects of my journey?

Integration occurs within all aspects of life. For Emma, integration came within a period of intense personal growth. This shift supported her to leave a toxic relationship and rediscover passions she had set aside. Through reflection, she connected her current sense of freedom to lessons learned during the difficult times. She created a series of doodles expressing her journey, transforming her emotions into smiles of release. This creative process and the silliness of the images allowed her to integrate her experiences, honoring both her struggles and her strength, fostering a deeper sense of wholeness.

Alignment: Living in Harmony

Alignment is the process of ensuring your outer actions reflect your inner truth. Like tuning a musical instrument, when the strings are properly adjusted, the music flows effortlessly – in alignment. Alignment is not about achieving a perfect balance but about creating a rhythm honoring both growth and rest.

Use these questions to reflect on how and what alignment is for you:

What's most important for me?

What self-beliefs empower my life?

How do my actions align with my deepest beliefs?

Through your awareness, picture yourself moving through a day where every decision reflects your truth. Initially there may be challenge as you consciously make this shift. Eventually you can imagine the ease and clarity of living in the balance of alignment.

Put your awareness on paper by listing all major commitments and evaluate their alignment with your principles. For each commitment, ask:

Is this commitment in alignment with my inner truth?

What can I release to create more harmony within me and my life?

Design intentional practices such as lighting a candle each morning to symbolize your commitment to alignment or setting affirmations that connect you with your calling.

To check in with yourself, ask:

How does my current alignment reflect my deepest values?

What commitments feel most aligned with my truth, and which ones need reassessment?

In what ways do my daily actions support my Soul Calling, Vision, and Paradox?

Sophia found herself constantly busy but unfulfilled. After reassessing her commitments and intentions, she realized that creativity and family were her highest priorities, yet her schedule left little room for either. She decided to realign her commitments, by setting aside one evening a week for family art time. This shift brought a sense of ease and connection back into her life, as she made the effort to realign commitment with importance.

Soul Compass Connections

Your Soul Compass process utilizes each of these pathways in your journey. Soul Compass is a practical process for navigating daily challenges and decisions and works through the connected awareness to your essential self. Each pathway supports the clarity, perspective, and actionable steps needed to deal with life transitions or moments of uncertainty. Here are some ways to apply the Soul Compass in your daily life.

For example, awareness can assist in identifying misalignment. Take a moment to notice where your current actions or relationships feel out of sync with your truth. For example, if a decision leaves you feeling drained or uneasy, reflect on what aspects of it conflict with your truth.

Transformation helps you embrace change by viewing shift as opportunities for growth. For instance, during a career change, reflect on what new perspectives or skills you can develop to move forward rather than focusing on what you are leaving behind.

Alignment helps to ensure that your daily actions consciously reflect your long-term vision. Break larger goals into smaller, manageable steps. Focus on creating actionable steps which you can easily incorporate into the natural flow of your life.

Integration assists in processing overwhelming emotions and finding connection in times of stress and overwhelm. Reflect on what lessons the stress is teaching you, and then find a small ritual – like lighting a candle or taking a mindful walk – to connect yourself to the present moment.

By returning to your essential self within these pathways, you can navigate challenges with trust and intention. Soul Compass helps you make decisions honoring your truth, whether you're choosing a new direction in life or simply seeking balance in a busy day.

The Dynamic Nature of Growth

Personal growth is not linear. Like with all of life, growth is a spiral path deepening your connection to your essential self with each turn. As new challenges and opportunities arise, revisiting earlier lessons provides fresh perspectives and insights, enriching your understanding and fostering continued evolution.

Each pathway plays a role in this cyclical process. For example, awareness invites you to observe recurring patterns in your thoughts and behaviors, revealing layers of insight that might not have been apparent before. Whereas, transformation challenges you to revisit past changes, understanding how they've reshaped your awareness and prepared you for new opportunities.

Encouraging you to weave these new understandings into your daily life, integration creates harmony between your past experiences and current aspirations. Joining together, alignment ensures that these insights guide your present actions, reinforcing your connection to your essential self.

Growth can also be acknowledged by returning to earlier lessons. For example, reflect on a decision made during a period of uncertainty and recognize how it set the stage for growth you hadn't anticipated. Revisiting these moments can assist you. Bringing awareness of the past into the present helps identify new layers of meaning. Insights that once seemed simple may take on deeper significance as you evolve. This intentional awareness can also assist in recognizing patterns. You can notice patterns spanning different phases of your journey, helping you understand how your path has unfolded. Plus, the expansion within awareness builds confidence. By acknowledging how past challenges prepared you for current ones you strengthen your trust in your process of growth.

By embracing this dynamic and spiral nature of growth, you allow your Soul Compass to guide you toward a life of ongoing discovery and authentic expression.

Embracing Your Journey

Take a moment to close your eyes and imagine standing at a rise in your road. The horizon ahead is the current direction of your journey, illuminated by the light of your Soul Compass. Reflect on how far you've come – the lessons you've learned, the growth you've embraced, and the awareness you've cultivated.

Feel the earth beneath your feet, solid and connecting, while the air around you carries a sense of possibility and renewal. Imagine stepping forward on this path, each step guided by the presence of your essential self. Trust that the journey ahead will unfold with clarity and intention, as you continue to honor your truth.

When you are ready, return to this present moment. Carry with you the sense of ease, balance, and calling which comes from living in alignment with your essential self. Know this connection to your presence will always guide you, no matter where life leads.

In this moment,

I embrace the pathways of my journey

to support my continuing process

of being and becoming.

5

LIVING WITHIN INNER TRUTH

In this moment,
I trust myself to open to the infinite flow
of my inner truth.

LIVING WITHIN INNER TRUTH BEGINS WHEN YOU DARE TO ALIGN YOUR daily choices with the deepest essence of who you are – the unique combination of your intention, desire, passion, and the quiet voice within whispering your calling. This is your essential self, the foundation upon which inner truth rests, waiting to be expressed with courage and intention.

Most importantly, inner truth isn't shaped by external expectations or the opinions of others. Your inner truth is found within you as a quiet steady voice reflecting your depth and understanding. Personal truth, voice of truth, my truth – these are the phrases to describe your awareness of the inner truth found within the depths of you.

Inner truth as a foundation, is neither absolute nor immovable. Truth evolves as you navigate the experiences of life, revealing new layers of understanding as you grow. Think of inner truth as a tree, its core solid and unchanging, but with each passing year, it adds rings of growth. These rings represent the wisdom and perspective gained through life's challenges and triumphs, making your inner truth richer and more nuanced over time.

When you live from inner truth, you begin to navigate life from the inside out. This means your choices, relationships, and actions stem from what is true within you, instead of being dictated by the demands and opinion of external authority. Imagine stepping into a stream flowing from deep within you, carrying your essential self to touch every aspect of your life. Living this way fosters a sense of wholeness and clarity, enabling you to move through life with trust and courage while remaining open to the evolution of your truth.

To connect with your inner truth, picture your life as a vast, intricate tapestry – each thread representing the many aspects and awarenesses of your truth. Threads like honesty, creativity, and compassion form the foundation of this design, influencing how your life unfolds. Honesty expresses as sturdy warp threads, providing structure and stability. Creativity emerges within the vibrant weft threads, adding color and dynamism, while compassion acts as the soft embellishments, creating depth and warmth.

However, it's not simply about honesty – it's about integrity. When you live within inner truth, your actions resonate with the agreements you've made with yourself and others. Integrity becomes the bridge between what you know in your heart and how you express in the world. Think of your forest, the sunlight breaking through the canopy, each ray illuminating your path. This light is your inner truth, unwavering even when shadows linger nearby.

Living within personal truth aligns the flow of your inner energy with the rhythms of the world around you, much like a river finding its natural course. When your choices resonate with your essential self, you feel a profound sense of harmony and ease, as though life itself is flowing effortlessly. Yet, like a tapestry, threads can become tangled or frayed. Intentional actions – reflecting, recalibrating, and reaffirming your truth – are the repairs restoring the integrity and beauty of your life's design.

Living from Inner Truth

Your inner truth is the core of your being – your essential self. Inner truth is what remains steady amidst life changes. Think of your life as a garden where your inner truth is the rich fertile soil. Without it, growth is shallow and unsustainable. With it, your life flourishes, each choice a seed planted in alignment with your calling.

Living from inner truth requires cultivating a deep connection with yourself. This involves listening, trusting, and acting in harmony with the voice of your power within. Within personal truth, you make decisions honoring your truth, even when truth challenges societal norms or external demands.

Imagine the feeling of relief and joy when your actions align with what truly matters *to you*. Like stepping into sunlight after a long winter, you experience a warmth and clarity touching every part of your life. This sensation of being connected yet limitless is rooted in who you are while being open to the infinite possibilities of you can become.

Take a moment to reflect on what inner truth feels like within you. Perhaps it manifests as a sense of calm, a spark of inspiration, or a quiet knowing. By tuning into these feelings, you strengthen your ability to recognize and act on your truth. Over time this connection empowers personal trust, compassion, and integrity.

Living inside out is a commitment to letting your inner truth guide both your inner landscape and your external life. This commitment creates harmony between what you feel, believe, and do. Inner truth then is the foundation of alignment, learning, and the integration of life's experiences.

To deepen this practice, know your inner truth is the steady, reliable foundation of your Soul Compass. For example, before deciding, pause and ask yourself:

Does this choice align with the essence of who I am?

This simple moment of reflection bridges the gap between inner clarity and external action, empowering you to live a life reflecting your soul's deepest intentions.

Additionally, truth is closely intertwined with intuition. Think of your intuition as a vital element of your Soul Compass, pointing toward resonant choices of your deepest self. While logic typically seeks certainty, intuition invites you to trust the quiet knowing within. Consider moments when you've followed your gut – perhaps a career choice that defied expectations but felt undeniably right, or a friendship you nurtured because something about it simply clicked. These instances illuminate truths logic might overlook, guiding you toward a more aligned and authentic path.

Overcoming the Cloud of Doubt

Doubt is one of the most pervasive barriers to living from inner truth. Clouding clarity, doubt makes it difficult to discern the steady voice of truth from the noise of uncertainty. Doubt arises from external pressures including societal expectations, conflicting advice, or fear of making the wrong choice. But it can also stem from within as your mind questions the validity of what your heart knows to be true.

Think of doubt as the fog settling over a path. The path is still there, but its details are cloaked. Doubt left to linger unchecked leads to hesitation, second guessing, and a disconnection from your inner truth. However, doubt also offers an opportunity for growth. By questioning and examining your doubts, you can deepen your understanding of your truth and strengthen your commitment to living inside out.

To navigate doubt, start by acknowledging its presence without judgment. Reflect on its source. Perhaps your doubt is rooted in a fear of failure, a desire to please others, or uncertainty about your next step. Once you identify its origins, ask yourself.

What does my inner truth tell me about my doubt in this moment?

What do I choose when I trust myself fully?

Over time you'll find doubt, rather than being an obstacle, becomes a guide. Doubt as paradox points you towards areas where your inner truth needs more attention or clarity, transforming uncertainty into new doorways to deeper self-awareness and alignment.

Confronting the Shadows of Fear

Fear is also a formidable barrier to inner truth, acting has a dark shadow clouding clarity and preventing action. Just as a shadow is not a tangible barrier and more a limiting perspective, fear emerges from the way you perceive the risks of embracing your truth. Fear warns you of potential risk and urges caution. Fear also looms large, distorting the view of your path ahead and making challenge seem insurmountable.

Fear also wants to manifest as a protective mechanism. However, instead of guiding, fear can trap you in a cycle of hesitation and avoidance. Yet, the shadow of fear, cannot exist without the light of truth. By shifting your perspective and moving closer to your inner truth, you begin to shrink the shadow, revealing a clear and steady path forward.

Fear whispers that your truth might disrupt relationships, challenge norms, or lead to failure. These whispers make it difficult to trust the quiet voice of inner truth within. When fear takes hold, you are disconnected from the steady foundation of your inner truth, leaving you vulnerable to external influences and self-doubt.

The connection between fear and inner truth is like the push and pull of a tide. Fear pulls you away, urging retreat from self. Inner truth calls you inward as a rhythmic wave returning always to the shore.

The tension between these forces is a dynamic process, inviting you to find balance and move with intention. When you recognize fear as part of the journey rather than the end of it, you can use it as a guide, uncovering the areas where your truth is most transformative and necessary. This reframing turns fear from a barrier into a compass, pointing towards the places where courage is needed to honor your depth and calling.

When fear surfaces, inner truth plays a crucial role in establishing personal boundaries. Fear tempts you to compromise your truth to maintain harmony or avoid conflict. However, this sacrifice can leave you feeling disconnected from yourself. Boundaries rooted in inner truth serve as acts of self-respect, allowing you to honor what aligns with your calling while communicating your needs with clarity and compassion. Imagine these boundaries is a protective yet flexible framework, one shielding your truth without isolating you from meaningful connection. By confronting fear and trusting your truth, you create a foundation where both your well-being and relationships can thrive.

The connection between fear and doubt amplifies their influence. While doubt clouds the path by questioning the validity of your truth, fear intensifies the fog by adding an emotional weight that can immobilize you. Together, they create a resistance to living inside out. Yet, fear also offers an opportunity for growth when approached with curiosity. By acknowledging fear without judgment, you begin to unravel its origins and understand its lessons. When you confront fear with resilience and courage, fear transforms from an obstacle into a catalyst, strengthening your connection to your truth and empowering you to act with integrity.

Navigating Barriers to Inner Truth

Resiliency and courage play vital roles in counteracting fear and doubt.

Resilience allows you to navigate these moments with grace and ease. Resiliency is the capacity to recover and realign with your inner truth when external pressures or internal uncertainties arise. By anchoring yourself in your inner truth, you create a strong foundation that helps you weather life's challenges without losing sight of what matters most. Like a tree with deep roots, resilience enables you to bend without breaking, maintaining your alignment even in turbulent times.

Courage complements resiliency by empowering you to take bold steps toward living inside out. Courage invites you to face fear directly, trusting your inner truth will guide you through the unknown. Each act of courage, no matter how small, strengthens your connection to your truth and reinforces your ability to live empowered Your courage is a bridge between doubt and clarity, enabling you to step forward with confidence and trust.

Courage emerges from inner truth as you embrace the vulnerability required to live truthfully. Acting from your inner truth often means stepping into the unknown or challenging societal norms, but it also opens the door to greater freedom and self-expression. Your inner truth is a steady flame – small at first and growing brighter each time you take a courageous step. Each act of bravery, no matter how small, strengthens your ability to trust yourself and deepens your alignment with your Soul Calling.

Together, resiliency and courage transform fear and doubt into opportunities for growth. They remind you that challenges are not obstacles but pathways to deeper self-awareness and alignment. By cultivating these qualities, you can protect and nurture the flame of your inner truth, ensuring it continues to guide you with clarity and calling.

Authenticity and Its Connection to Inner Truth

Authenticity is living in the world in alignment with your inner truth. Expressing your inner truth outwardly creates a bridge connecting who you are within to how you engage with the world. To be authentic means to act, speak, and live in ways reflecting your deepest intentions and inner truth, unhindered by societal expectations or external pressures.

Inner truth forms the foundation of authenticity. Without a connection to your inner truth, authenticity becomes a hollow ideal, subject to the shifting sands of external validation. By living inside out, rooted in your inner truth, you can approach life with a sense of wholeness and integrity. Authenticity becomes not just a goal but a natural extension of your inner truth.

Imagine your inner truth as the roots of a tree and authenticity as the fruit. When the roots are nurtured and strong, the fruit is abundant and nourishing. Likewise, when you live from your inner truth, your authentic self shines through effortlessly, creating deeper connections and fostering trust with those around you.

Living authentically requires courage and fosters resiliency. It means embracing vulnerability and being willing to let others see the unfiltered version of yourself. This openness fosters connection and inspires others to do the same, creating a ripple effect of authenticity that begins with your commitment to living from your inner truth.

Soul Compass Perspective of Inner Truth

Inner truth is the foundation and touchstone for every aspect of Soul Compass. Each element draws upon your awareness and your openness to the evolving nature of your inner truth.

Soul Calling, by definition, is the voice of your inner truth, pointing you toward what you are here to do and who you are here to become. By anchoring decision in inner truth, you align with the unique pull of your Soul Calling, allowing it to guide you toward choices reflecting your essential self.

When you consider your options, notice which path resonates most with your sense of meaning and direction. To meet challenge around calling, ask these questions of inner truth:

Does this choice align with my inner truth?

How does this awareness resonate with my inner truth?

In contrast, Soul Paradox reveals the richness of inner truth by inviting you to see challenge as opportunity and move beyond the *seeming* limits of contradiction. Apparent contradictions such as freedom and responsibility, or independence and connection become sources of wisdom when viewed through the lens of inner truth. Living inside out means not resolving these tensions but learning to hold them as complementary forces that deepen your self-understanding. Every choice holds layers of complexity.

Reflect on how freedom and responsibility, independence and connection, or other *seeming* opposites inform your decision and expand your understanding. For example, to find truth within paradox, ask these questions:

Am I rising above the contradictions within this decision?

What is my truth within this contradiction?

This sets the stage for your Soul Vision to expand your inner truth into a broader context. Connecting your daily actions with a larger narrative, vision allows you to see how living from your truth not only transforms your own life but also opens the door to new possibility and expanded opportunity. By reflecting on your Soul Vision, you can begin to understand how the small, intentional steps you take today build a future aligned with your calling. Here are several questions to ferret out deeper meaning of vision:

How does this decision contribute to the truth of my Soul Vision?

Does this vision honor my inner truth?

Will this action bring me closer to my Soul Vision?

Thus, inner truth is the thread weaving these three Soul Compass elements together, creating a dynamic and evolving guide for navigating life's complexities. As you engage with each element of Soul Compass, you deepen your connection to your inner truth and strengthen your trust in living inside out.

The Dynamic Bond Between Truth and Trust

The existence of inner truth rests within its own paradox: you must trust yourself to hear truth, yet trusting yourself requires a sense of personal truth.

This delicate balance reveals the interconnected nature of truth and trust, where one cannot exist fully without the other. Truth and trust are like the roots and branches of a tree – each supports the other, growing stronger and more expansive as the connection deepens. As inner truth deepens, personal trust grows in tandem, creating a feedback loop fortifying both. As you begin to trust your ability to discern and act on your truth, you set in motion a cycle of growth where each decision made from truth strengthens your relationship with yourself and deepens your ability to trust yourself.

Doubt and fear, however, often disrupt this cycle, acting as barriers to trust. Doubt whispers that your truth may be unreliable or inadequate, sowing uncertainty making it harder to trust your inner voice. Fear amplifies these doubts, warning of potential risks like rejection, disapproval, or failure. Together, doubt and fear create a haze obscuring your ability to see and act from your truth. This disconnect can leave you feeling paralyzed or swayed by external influences, undermining your sense of self-trust.

Courage and resiliency are the antidotes to this challenge, offering pathways to rebuild and expand trust. Courage allows you to take bold steps toward honoring your truth, even when fear and doubt loom large. Each act of bravery, no matter how small, reinforces your ability to trust yourself, proving that you can navigate challenges while staying aligned with your values. Resiliency complements courage by helping you recover and learn from moments when doubt or fear might momentarily derail you. Together, courage and resiliency transform obstacles into opportunities for deeper alignment with your truth.

As trust in your inner truth grows, so does your capacity to embrace the paradox of truth and trust. You begin to understand that doubt and fear are not signs of failure but invitations to strengthen the foundation of your trust. Over time, this expanded trust enables you to navigate life's complexities with clarity and confidence, making decisions reflecting the essence of who you are. The connection between truth and trust becomes a dynamic, evolving process, allowing you to meet each new challenge with a deeper sense of integrity and self-awareness.

The Evolving Nature of Inner Truth

Your inner truth is both unchanging and evolving. At its core, its presence remains steady, providing a foundation for your life. Yet, as you grow, your understanding of truth deepens. Life experience acts as a mirror reflecting back new dimensions of who you are and why you are here. This evolution is not a contradiction but a testament to the dynamic nature of being human.

Like a river, your source of inner truth is constant and its flow changes with the seasons, adapting to the terrain. The river bends around obstacles, carves new paths through rock, and carries sediments enriching its depth over time. Transitions, such as career changes, relationships, or significant losses, act like tributaries joining the river, adding complexity and richness to its course. In moments of stillness, the river pools, inviting reflection and quiet discovery before continuing its journey.

Major life phases, such as entering parenthood, stepping into a new career, or navigating the changes of aging, reveal entirely new layers of your inner truth. These phases act as inflection points, inviting you to reevaluate and reconnect with what matters most. Each transition brings opportunities for growth, as the flow of your inner truth adapts to meet the demands of the moment.

Another perspective is to see evolving truth as a kaleidoscope. With each shift in perspective, entirely new patterns and colors emerge, reflecting the multifaceted nature of your soul's journey. This transformation highlights the beauty and complexity of living inside out.

Plus, living inside out means revisiting your inner truth regularly, allowing its guidance to evolve as you do. Life milestones such as moving to a new home, starting a family, or stepping into a new role, offer opportunities to reconnect with your truth. In moments of doubt, take a pause to ask:

What has this experience revealed about my inner truth?

How is this experience or insight inviting me to grow?

This practice fosters resilience and adaptability, enabling you to align with your truth even as circumstances shift. To stay connected with the evolving nature of your truth, periodically reflect on these questions:

What does my inner truth ask of me in this season of life?

What lessons from past truths continue to shape me today?

How can I honor the evolution of my truth in my actions today?

By embracing the evolving nature of inner truth, you create space for transformation and integration while remaining anchored in the essence of who you are.

Inspiring Others by Living Inside Out

When you live from your inner truth, you become a source of inspiration. Your courage to align your outer life with your inner reality encourages others to do the same. Your actions create ripples, inviting those around you to explore their own truths.

Consider Elizabeth, who left a high-paying job to follow her passion for writing. Her decision inspired her friend Sophia to listen to her own inner truth. Or James, whose choice to innovate in his business encouraged his employees to embrace their creativity. Living inside out is not only transformative for you but also for those whose lives you touch.

Closing Reflection

Living from inner truth is not about perfection but about alignment. This is about letting the voice within guide you, trusting your inner truth as the compass that will always point you toward your vision. This journey is a continuous unfolding, a practice of deep listening and courageous action transforming not only your life but also the world around you.

Take a deep breath. Place your hand on your heart. Feel the steady rhythm connecting you to your essential self. Ask yourself:

What is my inner truth guiding me to do today?

Allow this question to settle, inviting clarity and insight to rise gently. Trust the answer, no matter how small or bold it feels. Recognize that each step guided by your truth is a thread weaving the tapestry of your authentic life in trust and alignment.

As the lighthouse of your essential self, your inner truth illuminates your path. With each decision, you deepen the channels of trust in yourself. Even when the waters feel uncertain, know your truth is steadfast, capable of guiding you through every twist and turn.

Let your life flow from the inside out. Be patient with the process, honoring both the still moments and the rushing currents. Trust that by aligning with your truth, you are contributing to a world where truth and courage inspire transformation and integration. As you live this truth, you become a beacon for others.

You open your door to new experiences as you transform, integrate, and align with the inner truth of your essential self.

In this moment,

I trust my inner truth to guide me.

6

OVERCOMING THE MYTH OF SOUL PURPOSE

*In this moment,
I find meaning in my process of
personal trust and inner truth.*

IN THIS MOMENT, SEE YOURSELF AT A VAST CROSSROADS OF MANY PATHS. Some paths are some well-trodden, while others are barely visible. A gentle breeze carries the scent of wildflowers and earth, filling the air with both possibility and uncertainty.

This is the moment where the myth of a singular soul purpose begins to unravel.

Life is not about finding the *one right* path. Rather, life is about listening inward, aligning with your truth, and stepping forward with courage and trust.

The Allure and Pressure of a Single Purpose

One of the most pervasive ideas in modern spirituality and self-help is the concept of a single life purpose – a predetermined reason for your existence, once discovered, unlocks all meaning and success.

This notion, while alluring, can also feel like chasing a mirage in the desert. The closer you think you are, the more it eludes you, leaving behind a sense of unworthiness and failure.

The search for soul purpose can feel like carrying a heavy weight – a backpack filled with the load of expectation and self-doubt. Each step forward becomes harder, the pressure to do perfectly stifling your ability to explore or experiment. Like wandering in an endless desert, each step drains your energy as hope fades into the horizon. Each step forward becomes harder, the pressure to *be right* stifling your ability to explore or experiment.

One of the foundational concepts of Soul Compass offers an alternative.

As calling, purpose is not a singular destination.

Calling is a dynamic process, unfolding in layers like the petals of a flower. Calling evolves as you do, shaped by the choices you make, the experiences you live, and the truths you uncover about yourself. By embracing this perspective, you free yourself from the myth of perfection and open to the richness of your evolving journey.

The Trap of Destination Thinking

Further, the idea of soul purpose is rooted in destination thinking: the belief that fulfillment rests in achieving a specific outcome or reaching a pre-determined, fixed point in life. Imagine climbing a mountain, convinced that the view from the top will solve all your problems, only to find another peak in the distance. This mindset assumes struggle will cease and everything will align once you *arrive*.

In reality, this perspective creates an impossible standard, leaving you chasing fulfillment always just out of reach.

Soul Compass reframes this narrative. Life is not a straight climb or a static destination. Life is fluid and ever-changing, like a river winding through valleys and over rocks.

Just as a river adapts to the terrain it encounters, carving new paths while flowing forward, your sense of purpose, your calling, evolves with the landscape of your experiences.

Purpose – intention, objective, goal, mission – is not found at a single endpoint but discovered in the movement of life itself. Each turn of your path brings you back to familiar themes, adding new layers of understanding and perspective.

Purpose as calling evolves in this same way, deepening with each cycle of growth. When you focus entirely on externalized goals, you risk losing connection with the present moment and essential self, delaying the truthful experience of happiness and fulfillment.

Additionally, purpose as destination is also hooked into a belief that the future is all – that the future is the only destination where all is guaranteed and fulfilled. If you successfully retrieve your purpose only then are you capable of getting to the promised perfect future. To achieve this success, you must disconnect from the present experience of your life, abandon personal truth as guide, and rely on external validation and approval.

However, the future is false destination if the goal is to believe in yourself and your calling – to trust you can create your life for you. Soul Compass invites you to release the need for a final destination and instead embrace the process of discovering, redefining, and living your calling in each moment.

Purpose as a Process

Given this expanded perspective of purpose as calling, rather than asking, "What is my purpose?" consider this question instead:

In this moment, how can I align with my truth right now?

This question will take you down the less traveled path and open doors to unseen possibility. As you begin this new journey, reinforce trust by taking a moment to reflect and ask these questions:

What beliefs have shaped my understanding of purpose?

How might beliefs about purpose be limiting my ability to embrace the possibilities of my journey?

Reflecting on these questions can help shift your perspective and find alignment in the present moment. This subtle shift transforms purpose from a static ideal into an active practice. Purpose as a process of Soul Calling becomes less about finding the *one perfect thing* you are meant to do. As calling you begin to explore how you can express your truth and follow a life path filled with the achievement of your vision in each moment.

Imagine purpose as a mosaic, each tile representing a choice, an experience, or a moment of alignment. Each tile is unique – some vivid and bright, others muted or unexpected. However, together they form an intricate design, telling the story of your evolving life. This mosaic grows as you do, expanding with every new insight and experience, creating a masterpiece that is uniquely yours. Some tiles shimmer with vibrant hues, representing moments of clarity and alignment, while others are muted, reflecting quieter periods of growth and reflection. Some have the ragged edges of challenge and disappointment. Together, they create a masterpiece of infinite depth and beauty. This mosaic is dynamic, expanding and evolving as you grow.

Transformed through Soul Compass, purpose becomes a process of living, expressed through the journey and application of Soul Calling and Soul Vision. By focusing on alignment in the present moment, you naturally move toward fulfilling your evolving sense of purpose as calling.

Seen through the lens of Soul Compass, purpose as calling evolves as a focus about living with intention and integrity. You feel called to make choices aligned with who you are and the expression of your inner truth. This means your purpose can and will change as you grow, as your circumstances evolve, and as your understanding of yourself deepens.

For example, you may feel called to one path during a particular phase of life – raising a family, pursuing a career, or exploring creative passions – only to find that calling shift as new experiences and insights emerge. Imagine a gardener who cultivates one vibrant flowerbed in spring but shifts attention to planting a new crop in summer. Each phase serves a purpose, contributing to the beauty and abundance of the garden as a whole. Each phase aligned with the natural cycles of creation and experience. This doesn't mean you were wrong in spring. Rather, you are learning you are adaptable, responsive, and alive to the possibilities of your journey unfolding in the moment.

Releasing the Pressure of Perfection

The myth of soul purpose carries with it an undercurrent of pressure and perfectionism. You may worry that if you don't discover your purpose, you are failing in some fundamental way. This fear can feel like being lost in a dense fog, unable to see the path ahead or trust your steps.

Soul Compass encourages you to release this pressure by embracing the idea that purpose as calling is not a single answer but a series of choices. Letting go of the pressure to *get it right* feels like exhaling after holding your breath for far too long. This is liberation inviting you to explore with curiosity and joy. Imagine putting down that heavy suitcase you've towed for years, filled with the expectations of others and the burden of outdated beliefs. With each step forward, you feel lighter, freer to explore the open possibilities ahead.

See yourself navigating a maze, each turn revealing new possibilities rather than dead ends. Mistakes, detours, and uncertainty are integral parts of the process and not signs of failure. Like a sculptor working with raw stone, each strike of the chisel might feel uncertain. However, every mark contributes to revealing the masterpiece within. These moments of trial and error refine your understanding and bring your calling into clearer focus.

Plus, challenges often reflect Soul Paradox, moments where fears and assumptions arise to test your resolve. By confronting and working through them, you transform obstacles into opportunities for growth, deepening your alignment with your evolving calling.

Each choice, even those which *seem* wrong, contributes to your growth and understanding. By reframing purpose as a journey rather than a destination, you give yourself permission to experiment, to learn, and to evolve. You step with confidence into the natural cycles of life and embrace the ebb and flow with trust established and truth believed. Life as a garden changes with the seasons and each bloom reflects the care and attention you bring to it. Your purpose, your calling, like this garden, grows richer and more colorful as you nurture yourself over time. Your spiral deepens and casts itself into the stars, into the galaxies, and into the mysteries of the transcendent.

The Freedom of Multiple Possibilities

One of the most liberating aspects of purpose as calling is the realization that there is not just one path to fulfillment. Your possibilities are endless and the direction you take is your choice. There are countless ways to express your calling, and all are valid. You might find fulfillment through relationships, through work, through creativity, or simply through the way you choose to show up in the world.

This openness to multiple possibilities allows you to approach life with curiosity rather than rigidity, to approach with eagerness than reticence. To explore this, take a moment to ask:

What roles, experiences, or passions have felt most meaningful to me?

What threads connect moments of meaning?

How do the threads and the moments contribute to the evolving mosaic of my calling?

This reflection can help uncover patterns and possibilities aligned with your unique journey. Reflecting on these threads can help you uncover the mosaic of your unique journey. Instead of asking, Am I doing the right thing? you can ask:

What feels true and meaningful to me in this moment?

This question brings you back to your inner compass, helping you navigate life with greater ease and trust.

Embracing Your Evolving Purpose as Calling

No longer bound by the need for external validation, as you move forward, remember purpose is not something you find once and for all. A purposeful life is a process you live into, moment by moment, choice by choice. Purpose, as Soul Calling, is shaped by your experiences, your relationships, and your willingness to listen to your truth. By embracing this dynamic view of purpose, you free yourself from the constraints of *getting it right* and open yourself to the joy of discovery in the moment.

Purpose is not a static answer. Rather finding purpose is a living process, one deeply connected to the interplay of Soul Calling, Soul Paradox, and Soul Vision, reinforcing the central approach of Soul Compass.

As you align with your truth, trust your path will unfold within the power of the unknown. Let the evolving rhythm of your path guide you, one step at a time as you trust your choices for a life of alignment and discovery.

No longer tied to destination, learning peace with seeing just a few steps ahead, you trust your inner awareness and your truth as it calls to you.

This is the power of Soul Compass: to guide you not to a fixed destination, instead to a life of ongoing alignment, growth, and empowerment.

In each moment,

my life is guided by a

deepening awareness of

alignment, growth, and empowerment.

7

THE PRIMARY QUESTIONS

In this moment,
my questions open the door to
my life's most exciting possibility.

THE HEART OF YOUR SOUL COMPASS RESTS WITHIN THIS ONE SIMPLE YET profound truth:

The questions you ask shape your inner dialogue and point towards the path you will choose.

More than tools for gathering information, questions are keys unlocking the hidden door of personal understanding. Like a beam of light illuminating what once was shadowed, you are invited to perceive life with greater clarity and within new perspective.

Asking a question opens the door of possibility. A dialogue begins. In this process of inquiry is the opportunity to receive what was once unknown. In questioning, you go beyond the inherent limits within your thinking and break down barriers to slight nuance and profound shift. Each question reveals new roads and broader opportunity than what personal perception held within the previous moment.

In life, there is a constant motion between what you know and what you don't. When you come to a standstill, when you're not sure of your next step, it's time to shift some aspect of the unknown into conscious awareness.

Questions are the door between the known and the unknown. When you ask a question, you signal your readiness and your point of self-responsibility. When you ask you are saying: *I am ready to receive from the unknown. I'm ready to understand what I don't know.*

Within all the fears of life and within all the pushes to be perfect, questions get caught in the demand. Thus, the search becomes the *one right* question to yield the *one right* answer. As if within infinite possibility only one is relevant.

Yet in the pursuit of the *one right* question, life shifts from receiving personal truth and gets stuck in a pointless search for something without true personal meaning.

Remember, the point of any question is the dialogue process opened within the inquirer. Life isn't about the *one right* – rather life is a continual process of inquiry and discovery.

Questions open the door. When you can dodge fear, uncertainty, and the demand for perfection, you enter into the dialogue between you, your essential self, and your connection with all that is known, unknown and unknowable.

In the context of your Soul Compass, questions are not about finding absolute answers. Rather questions invite you to the ongoing dialogue between your inner truth and the world around you.

Questions are touchstones to guide your journey, helping you navigate the complexities of life with integrity, courage, and resilience.

Primary Soul Compass Questions

Within Soul Compass there are four primary questions crafted to center your awareness, open your heart, and align your actions. Your goal is not the *one right* destination. Instead, Soul Compass is a process of attunement in each moment with inner truth as you move through life's ever-changing landscape.

The first three primary questions focus on the three elements of Soul Compass: Soul Calling, Soul Paradox, and Soul Vision. The fourth question continually turns the cycle of your life path and rotates your compass in new directions as you embrace the challenge and opportunity which naturally accompanies the process of life.

First Question: Soul Calling

In this moment, what is my Soul Calling?

This question identifies the deep truth of what you are called to be, do, or become in this moment. Encouraging connection with your inner personal truth, this question is applicable to life's broader arcs or to specific situations, projects, or timelines.

Second Question: Soul Paradox

What is the Soul Paradox of this calling?

This focuses on uncovering fears, beliefs, or assumptions which *seem* to hinder alignment with your Soul Calling. This is a question to explore what creates resistance or doubt, or hides denial or contradiction. The paradox rests in what *seems* to be insurmountable and actually when resolved is the bridge between calling and vision.

Third Question: Soul Vision

What is the Soul Vision aligned with my calling?

This question unites calling and paradox to find the path of truth for you. Whether the vision is clear or still unfolding, this inquiry supports trust in the unfolding process of vision while enabling actionable steps.

Fourth Question: Next Step

What is my next step?

This question distills process into immediate, actionable clarity and translates the overarching vision into tangible action aligned with your Soul Calling. This is the question to ask both when you come to a standstill and when you are ready to move forward. This is also the question pushing you, so you don't hold yourself back due to fear and worry. One step is all that is needed to begin. One step gets you out of inertia.

THESE FOUR PRIMARY QUESTIONS ARE NOT STATIC CHECKPOINTS BUT dynamic guides encouraging the cyclical process of reflection, alignment, and action. They create a rhythm harmonizing your inner truth with your daily life, and ensuring every step forward is intentional and meaningful.

While the primary questions begin your journey, they are not limited to any one point of your life. Instead, these questions create a continual cycle of ask, receive, and act. Each question creates an opening to new understanding and shifted perception. Each question moves you within the flow of your journey beyond the demands of perfectionism and control.

Most importantly, the four primary questions open doors for deeper inquiry and additional questions to help you come to an understanding of what fulfills the primary question. To get to a clear response to any of the four primary questions requires more questions. Each question drills down beyond the surface helping you put together a clearer picture.

Which questions to ask will depend on your focus and your calling. Different questions will arise depending on where you are within your vision and the phase of your paradox. What you ask and when will also directly relate to self-trust and self-understanding.

Getting Out of Overwhelm

This may seem overwhelming, yet it is a description of the continual thought work and heart work that is a constant companion on your life's journey. By identifying the three aspects which help you envision your life, Soul Compass questions empower you to trust yourself to live your life within this aligned vision.

Key to these questions is personal trust. Do you trust yourself to hear your inner truth? External demand wants to disempower and convince you that you can't trust yourself. Without trust, then believing your inner dialogue is difficult.

However, part of the power of Soul Compass comes in the repetition of questions. Each time you ask, you open the door to connect with your inner truth. Each question helps reinforce personal trust and opens self to expanded perception. Each question emerges within the inward journey along your spiral path.

Tuning Into Your Inner State

When you are uncertain about a response to a question, check in with yourself. Outdated habit, detrimental self-belief, and old stories will try to insert themselves and convince you self-trust is pointless and inner truth is faulty.

In the face of uncertainty, take a breath. Then ask a question about you. Check in with your emotions and thoughts. Questions provide a mirror reflecting your inner state. Remember, often it is the struggle in getting to an answer which reveals the path of release and the unfolding of vision. As in all life, questions are not about destination. Questions are the journey.

In uncertainty, the following questions will guide reconnection with yourself and re-ignite your inner dialogue. Each question can create a moment of clarity to allow your emotional and mental landscapes to come into focus. Each question can trigger release and momentary uncertainty allowing clarity to be revealed.

What is my truth now?

IN EACH MOMENT, YOUR AWARENESS OF YOUR INNER TRUTH IS YOUR guide. When you are uncertain, begin here. By asking this question you are checking in with yourself to see if disconnection from truth is the challenge.

What am I feeling right now?

THIS QUESTION INVITES YOU TO CONNECT YOURSELF WITH YOUR awareness of the present moment. Feelings are the language of the soul, offering clues to your inner state and pointing toward areas needing attention or celebration. By asking this question, you cultivate the practice of emotional awareness, which is essential for awareness, transformation, integration, and alignment.

What am I resisting?

RESISTANCE SIGNALS AREAS WHERE PERSONAL GROWTH OR transformation is needed. This question encourages you to examine what feels uncomfortable or challenging and to explore the underlying fears, beliefs, or patterns holding you back.

What am I longing for?

LONGING IS THE SOUL'S WAY OF GUIDING YOU TOWARD YOUR TRUEST desires and calling. By identifying what you deeply yearn for, you can align your actions with what truly matters, moving closer to a life of fulfillment and truth.

What does alignment feel like for me?

ALIGNMENT IS A DEEPLY PERSONAL EXPERIENCE UNIQUE TO EACH individual. This question encourages you to define and recognize the sensations, emotions, or thoughts signaling when you are in harmony with your soul's truth.

What step can I take right now?

INTEGRATION IS NOT ABOUT GRAND GESTURES BUT ABOUT CONSISTENT, meaningful action. A form of the fourth primary question, the intention is to connect insight and practical steps, reminding you even the smallest action can create ripples of transformation.

Threads of Transformation

These primary Soul Compass questions are not just tools for self-reflection, they are companions on your journey, guiding you toward greater clarity, integration, and alignment. They act as steady beacons, illuminating your inner truth and helping you navigate the vast terrain of your soul's calling.

By engaging with these questions consistently, you create a dynamic dialogue with your soul, one informing and enriching every aspect of your life. In their simplicity lies their power, offering a gentle yet profound invitation to step beyond the surface and uncover the truths hidden within.

With each question, you peel back another layer of resistance, fear, or doubt, discovering not only clarity but also the courage to embrace your authentic path. In their practice are the threads of your transformation, weaving together the fabric of your becoming. Here, you find not just answers, but a steady rhythm reconnecting you to the infinite possibilities of your essential self, allowing your soul's vision to unfold with grace.

In this moment,

I find joy in hearing my truth

within the questions I ask.

8

SOUL CALLING: HEARING YOUR INNER TRUTH

*In this moment,
I open my heart to hear my truth.*

DUSK AND THE SUN IS SETTING. YOU ARE WALKING THROUGH A DENSE forest, and the air is heavy with the earthy scent of moss and fallen leaves. The path ahead is unclear, cloaked in shadows and tangled roots. Then, faintly at first, you hear a whisper carried on the breeze, a gentle call stirring something deep within. The sound filters in a thread of light weaving through the dark canopy, pulling at your heart to follow a path still shadowed. You pause, opening to the sound, a mix of curiosity and anticipation drawing your attention and awareness.

This is the essence of Soul Calling – the quiet, persistent voice of your truth beckoning you to welcome alignment with who you are and who you can become. Hearing your Soul Calling can feel both exhilarating and tender, as if entering a warm beam of sunlight after a long-shadowed journey. Stirring emotions of vulnerability and excitement, you are invited to embrace the unknown with both courage and curiosity.

The Nature of Soul Calling

Soul Calling is not a command shouted from the mountaintop. Soul Calling is a whisper from the depths of your being. Subtle yet unmistakable, your calling is like the first light of dawn painting the horizon in hues of possibility. This calling emerges not from external expectations but from the sacred wellspring within you, inviting you to live in resonance with your essential self.

Soul Calling feels like an inner pull toward meaningful awareness, a tug of what lights you up and feels true. The pull of your calling may feel like standing on the edge of a vast canyon – thrilling yet daunting, inviting you to leap while testing your trust. It stirs both fear and excitement, a reminder that finding alignment with your truth often requires courage and vulnerability.

Soul Calling can feel like a push within to open your heart and clear your mind of the debris of life. This is a push to open to the flow of life within and acknowledge the connections of this flow with all of life.

Soul Calling is also a compass needle that quivers and steadies, pointing you toward your true north. Your calling can appear as the first bud of spring breaking through winter's hold, delicate yet full of promise. Sometimes Soul Calling arrives as a flutter of excitement when you think about a new opportunity or as a quiet certainty nudging you to explore an uncharted path. At times, calling feels like the gentle warmth of a spring breeze, and at others, the mighty roar of a storm, demanding your attention with urgency.

At its core, Soul Calling is dynamic, not static. It is a direct conduit to the awareness within you of both your expansive inner nature and your connection with the transcendent wonder of life. Soul Calling evolves as you grow, responding to your life's experiences and your expanding awareness. Each time you hear your calling, it may feel familiar yet new, like the refrain of a song you've always loved but are just now truly understanding.

What feels like your calling today might shift tomorrow as life experience deepens your understanding of yourself and the world around you. This fluidity can feel both liberating and challenging, but it is what keeps life's journey exciting and joyful.

Soul Calling is often experienced as a feeling of resonance or excitement within the core of your essential self. When you encounter an idea, project, or possibility singing with your truth, you feel or sense alignment. This calling can be subtle, like a quiet whisper tugging at the edges of your consciousness, or bold and urgent, demanding immediate attention and action. Regardless of its intensity, the experience of Soul Calling carries a sense of rightness, a knowing transcending logic or external validation.

At times, Soul Calling may feel elusive, especially when life's noise and distraction drown out your inner voice or when disappointment reinforces mistrust. Yet, this calling remains ever-present, waiting for moments of awareness to make itself known. The clarity of a calling may be immediate or unfold gradually, revealing itself layer by layer as you engage with the journey.

Your calling does not always come with detailed instructions or a clear path forward. Instead, it invites you to step into the unknown guided by trust: trust in yourself, trust in the process, and trust that the first step will lead to the next.

Embracing Soul Calling requires a willingness to be open, curious, and flexible. You are encouraged to live with intention and integrity, honoring your truth emerging from within while navigating the uncertainties of life.

Your Soul Calling is always in motion, evolving as you grow, and your understanding deepens. What resonates today may transform tomorrow, reflecting the ever-changing dance between your inner world and the external landscape. Yet, no matter its form, Soul Calling is always there, waiting for you to listen and respond by accepting the lead in your life's dance.

The Many Forms of Soul Calling

There is no one form of Soul Calling, nor in life is there just one Soul Calling for you. Once you open to the possibility, you will experience calling in all facets of life.

Some know from an early age the calling of the entire arc of their lives. Jess pushed through every obstacle and delay to become a doctor, satisfying a childhood dream. Each step forward came with moments of exhaustion, but also profound joy when she felt herself living her calling.

Or Meredith, who translated her early love of science fiction into best-selling fantasy novels in her early thirties. She found solace and excitement in crafting worlds reflecting her inner wonder, transforming her passion into stories with deep resonance.

Yet, for most, Soul Calling begins in one direction and quickly shifts as life experience brings new understanding and unimagined possibility.

For example, Lily, in her early twenties, felt a deep pull to become a teacher despite struggling in school as a child. This calling initially filled her with uncertainty and self-doubt, but also a quiet excitement giving her courage to pursue her dreams. After ten years of a fulfilling career in the classroom, she felt a new calling emerge – the urge to write a book and share her wisdom beyond the walls of her school. This transition was transformative, filling her with renewed purpose and the joy of expanding her impact. The transition felt both daunting and exhilarating, but as she followed her calling, she discovered a deeper awareness of alignment and trust.

Or think about Suzanne, who chose to study finance in college because it seemed practical and her parents approved. Yet, as she spent more time outdoors, she realized she was drawn to environmental efforts, not only because of her deep connection to nature but also because she wanted to help environmental organizations achieve financial stability. This blend of practicality and passion became a new avenue for her calling.

In contrast, at an early age John decided to follow in his father's footsteps and became an engineer. Yet, he found himself unfulfilled despite professional success. After volunteering at a community center teaching kids how to build model rockets, he realized his passion was education. This calling led him to leave his corporate job and start a STEM education program, finding joy and alignment in this new path.

Or take Maria, a graphic designer who burned out working on corporate branding projects. During a weekend nature retreat, she felt a pull to reconnect with her love of painting landscapes. Following this calling, she transitioned into freelance work, creating space for personal art projects that reignited her passion.

Finally, think about Rex, a busy parent who always dreamed of traveling but thought it impractical. Drawn to explore his ancestral roots, he began planning small trips with his family, weaving meaningful travel experiences into their lives. Along the way, the experience helped him learn how to prepare for the journey both literally and metaphorically. Along the way he created a family process which engaged everyone in the planning, gave each child a choice in trip activities, and helped him find deeper connection with his ancestry, his family, and himself.

Remember callings can emerge from unexpected places, evolve over time, and bring deeper meaning to life. This is a process not of one-time revelation but an ongoing dialogue with your inner self. Soul Calling evolves and adapts, guiding you through the many arcs and turns of your life.

Discovering Your Soul Calling

To hear your Soul Calling, quiet the noise of the world and turn inward. Imagine a still lake at dawn, its surface unbroken by ripples, mirroring the sky's vast expanse. Envision the noise of the world retreating into this stillness, leaving a space of calm and clarity. In the pause, your Soul Calling begins to emerge, steady and clear.

Or close your eyes and imagine standing in a peaceful forest. Quietly feel into the peace and ask:

What whispers or pulls are drawing me forward?

How do these feelings guide me toward alignment?

This simple visualization helps you connect with the quiet truth of your Soul Calling. This is the state of being which supports you as you tune into your calling – a state of presence, curiosity, and openness.

Remember, hearing your Soul Calling emerges within stillness and attentiveness. In a world filled with distractions, carving out moments of quiet reflection is essential. Reflect on a moment when you felt deeply alive and trace the themes within this memory. Consider how these themes connect to your present awareness of calling.

The point is to uncover patterns, guiding you closer to your truth. These moments allow you to tune into your inner voice and separate it from the noise of external expectation or inner fear.

The felt balance of resonance is one of the most profound ways to recognize your Soul Calling. Balance is the feeling or sense of deep alignment and balanced harmony with an idea, action, or possibility. When you encounter something resonating with your heart and soul, it feels unmistakable – a sense of rightness transcending logic. There can literally be a buzz felt inside when you feel the resonance of calling. This resonance often brings excitement, peace, or a quiet certainty, as if your whole being is saying, *YES, this is for me!*

Resonance can show up in subtle or unexpected ways. Some feel a gentle pull toward something meaningful while others experience an electrifying moment of clarity. Resonance appears in the unexpected – a conversation with a stranger, a passage in a book, or a fleeting thought during your morning walk. Paying attention to these moments helps you uncover the threads of your Soul Calling.

Learning to identify resonance requires practice. Listening not just with your mind but with your body and heart as well. Notice when you feel energized or uplifted. Notice where you experience a sense of ease or flow. Notice when the proverbial bulb lights up. These are clues to your Soul Calling. By tuning into resonance, you allow your inner truth to guide you toward the pathways of your presence.

Because Soul Calling is the voice of your truth, you do not, will not, have just one. Soul Calling follows the many arcs of your life. While you certainly can have a calling which spans your entire life, Soul Calling is more. Connected to all the shorter arcs such as the motion into a new year, the creation of a project, or the interaction with a partner or group, Soul Calling is in your presence and in your trust.

Thus, Soul Calling isn't a one-and-done activity. Rather Soul Calling is a process of guidance in each moment to help you create and live your life in alignment with dream, desire, and destiny.

Soul Compass Questions for Soul Calling

To connect with your Soul Calling, begin with this primary Soul Compass question:

What is my Soul Calling?

Direct, simple – ask in quiet times of reflection. Ask as you arise or as you sleep. Ask while you walk, drive, or do the dishes. When times are tough or you feel uncertain, take a deep breath and ask. The experience of asking will, over time, help you trust yourself to hear the response.

You can also focus this primary question in any direction. For example:

In this moment, what is my Soul Calling?

In my life, what is my Soul Calling?

In this project, what is my Soul Calling?

With this person, what is my Soul Calling?

As I make this fresh start, what is my Soul Calling?

Sometimes the response will be quick. Though more often questions ignite attention, and response takes a bit to bubble up into your awareness. Remember, this isn't about the *one right* answer. Rather your Soul Calling is your awareness of your truth in the moment of asking.

You can also get to Soul Calling by asking less direct questions including:

What brings me joy?

What feels meaningful to me right now?

What am I longing for?

These questions can help you uncover patterns and themes which point toward calling. This type of reflection can also create space for silence and mindfulness. Through focus, your mind quiets and you can listen deeply to the wisdom of your heart and soul.

Another approach to hearing Soul Calling is to notice what excites or energizes you. Pay attention to where you feel naturally drawn. Think about what activities or ideas spark a sense of excitement or alignment. Revisit past inspirations. Reflect on times in your life when you felt most alive or connected. Observe the themes or patterns which emerge. These moments often hold clues to your calling.

Navigating Resistance to Soul Calling

As your calling moves toward you, resistance may rise like a sudden headwind, chilling your resolve. Fear tightens in your chest, doubt whispers insidious questions, and old stories resurface, telling you why you can't or shouldn't. This resistance, though uncomfortable, is not a sign to stop. Resistance is a threshold to cross.

Feel the weight of resistance in your body – a knot in your stomach or a tightening in your throat. Name it, sit with it, and ask what it wants to teach you. Resistance often guards the door to your next level of growth, and by facing it, you unlock new layers of courage and clarity.

Responding to your Soul Calling can feel exhilarating, and can also stir up fear, doubt, and uncertainty. You may wonder if you are good enough, if the time is *right*, or if you're ready to take the leap. These feelings are natural and part of the process.

Resistance often arises from fears or limiting beliefs. You might feel pressure to conform to societal expectations or worry about how others will perceive your choices. These doubts can stem from cultural conditioning, past experiences, or fear of failure taking root over time. Recognize these patterns and allow yourself to challenge and release them, clearing the way for your Soul Calling to take center stage.

Resistance may also manifest as procrastination, perfectionism, or self-sabotage. For example, you might find yourself endlessly planning instead of acting or convincing yourself that other responsibilities must take precedence. Understanding these behaviors as protective mechanisms can help you approach them – and you – with compassion rather than judgment. When you acknowledge resistance is often that inner impulse attempting to keep you safe, you can begin to gently navigate through instead of holding yourself back

One way to work with resistance is to focus on small, actionable steps. Rather than attempting to tackle your calling all at once, identify a single step in the moment that feels manageable and achievable. By building momentum gradually, you can lessen the hold of fear and increase your confidence.

It's also helpful to remind yourself of your *why* – the *why* of your body, mind, heart, and soul:

> **Why does this Soul Calling matter to me?**

> **How will I feel to live aligned with my Soul Calling?**

Reconnecting with the deeper meaning behind your calling provides the motivation to move forward, even in the face of resistance. Focused on why loosens the edge of resistance and supports deeper inquiry. Already nudging your awareness into the contradictions of paradox, you can explore the layers of resistance to calling with these questions:

> **What fears surface when I consider following my Soul Calling?**

> **When I release the need for certainty, how can I move forward?**

Navigate Soul Calling by seeing resistance as guidance through the crossroads with the inner truth of your essential self in full view.

Living Aligned with Soul Calling

To live in alignment with your Soul Calling is to step into the flow of life where ease and intention converge. This is the experience of the river, its current strong yet graceful, bringing toward you awareness of your calling. When you align with your calling, you become like this river, moving with intention and trust.

Living your calling doesn't mean the path will always be smooth. Rapids will appear, demanding attention and courage. Yet even amidst challenge, the river of alignment flows to you, oriented by the resonance of your truth.

In each moment, when you align with Soul Calling, you begin to experience life with greater clarity and purpose. Your decisions become rooted in personal truth rather than external pressure and expectation. This alignment does not guarantee an easy path, but it does ensure a meaningful one.

Living within Soul Calling involves embracing resistance, moving beyond the push towards perfectionism, and trusting the unfolding process. You don't need to have every step mapped out. Start where you are, take the first step, and let the journey reveal itself as you go. Every action aligned with your calling strengthens your connection to your truth and deepens your sense of integration, alignment, and trust.

Know Soul Calling is not a one-time discovery but an ongoing dialogue within the awareness of your inner self. By staying attuned to this voice, you remain open to the possibilities life offers, engaging each moment within resonance and with courage.

Take small steps to honor your calling each day. Dedicate time to pursuits igniting your passion. In this flame is your calling.

Speak your truth in moments that matter. In this trust is the flow of your Calling.

Say no to what feels misaligned, creating space for what resonates. In this alignment is the power of your body, mind, heart, and soul – and the belief of you as the awesome person you are and are always becoming.

Picture your Soul Calling as a thread of light weaving through the tapestry of your life, connecting moments of wonder, challenge, and growth. Let the warmth of these threads guide you, step by step, toward your powerful essential self. Listen for the whisper of your truth, and let it guide you home.

Interweaving Soul Calling with Soul Paradox and Soul Vision

Soul Calling does not exist in isolation and is deeply connected with the other two elements of Soul Compass: Soul Paradox and Soul Vision. Together, these three form the dynamic process of Soul Compass, guiding you through the complexities of life with clarity and truth.

As a preview to the next chapter, know Soul Paradox arises as a direct response to your Soul Calling. When you feel the pull of your calling, paradox arises as resistance, fear, or doubt, creating the impression that your calling is unattainable or impractical. These moments are not obstacles to avoid but invitations to explore and resolve the fears or limiting beliefs holding you back. By addressing your Soul Paradox, you gain a deeper understanding of what stands in the way of your truth and how to move beyond it.

In contrast, Soul Vision transforms the clarity gained from resolving paradox into actionable steps. While Soul Calling identifies what resonates deeply within you, Soul Vision helps you see how to bring resonance into reality. Vision provides the pathway for aligning your actions with your calling, offering a sense of direction even when the way forward is uncertain. Soul Vision enables you to craft a life reflecting your truth and evolves with your growth.

The reciprocal exchange of these elements creates a continuous cycle of discovery, challenge, and fulfillment. Your calling draws you forward, your paradox tests and strengthens you, and your vision provides the means to embody your truth. Together, Soul Compass forms a holistic approach to living life within truth and vision.

The Cyclical Nature of Soul Calling

Not at all linear, Soul Calling is cyclical, evolving as you move through different phases of life. A vibrant and urgent calling today may shift or expand tomorrow as new experience and insight arise. This cyclical nature reflects the spiral path of personal growth, where each turn deepens your understanding and alignment.

You may revisit themes or ideas that felt resolved, only to discover new layers of meaning. For instance, someone called to teach may find their role evolves from classroom instruction to mentoring, writing, or advocacy. Similarly, a creative calling might expand from a personal hobby into a community initiative, reflecting a broader scope of impact.

This cyclical process encourages you to remain flexible and open. Rather than clinging to a fixed notion of your calling, you allow it to grow alongside you. Embracing this evolution helps you stay connected to your truth while honoring the changing landscape of your life.

A Final Invitation

Remember, Soul Calling is not a one-time discovery but an ongoing dialogue with your inner self through all the many motions of life. By staying attuned to your voice, you remain open to the possibilities life offers, navigating each moment with truth and trust. Your Soul Calling is unique, dynamic, and endlessly worth pursuing, across and within the many bends and turns of your life.

Your Soul Calling is not something to find *outside* of yourself – rather, Soul Calling is a revelation of you. Soul Calling is the thread woven through your life's tapestry, connecting moments of joy, curiosity, and growth. Listen for the whisper of your truth, and let this song guide you through uncertainty. Trust each step, no matter how small, as a sacred act of alignment.

Close your eyes and place your hand on your heart. Breathe deeply.

What truth is stirring within me right now?

What whispers are asking to be heard?

Follow. Listen to these whispers, the stirring in your heart. Listen to the voice of your Soul Calling to live with the power of your deepest inner truth. Your calling will connect you always with all of you, body, mind, heart, and soul.

In this moment,

I embrace Soul Calling

as the voice of

my deepest inner truth.

9

SOUL PARADOX: THE KEY TO UNLOCKING FEAR

*In this moment,
I am open to understanding
the challenges of my life's path.*

SOUL PARADOX IS THE CONFLICT WITH YOUR SOUL CALLING AND THE fear which *seems* to hold you back. Soul Paradox is the tension arising when your Soul Calling meets resistance, fear, or doubt. This paradox represents the moments when your inner truth feels at odds with external circumstances or internal insecurities.

The key here is *seems*. While paradox may *seem* like a roadblock, it is, in fact, an essential element of your journey. By engaging with your Soul Paradox, you uncover the beliefs and fears holding you back and transform them into opportunities for growth. That's the paradox: what *seems* to be a block is in effect, the bridge leading you to envision your Soul Calling.

Understanding Soul Paradox

Essentially, Soul Paradox is the *seeming* contradiction between the clarity of your calling and the challenges arising in pursuit. These moments of paradox are not barriers to your growth but invitations to uncover deeper truths about yourself.

For instance, you might feel a strong pull toward a new creative endeavor while simultaneously fearing the financial implications or doubting your talent. This tension highlights the interactions between your aspirations and the beliefs or fears which *seem* to limit you.

Paradox often reflects unresolved inner conflicts or competing priorities. You may desire freedom but fear instability. You might long for self-expression while craving external approval. These conflicts are natural and universal, reminding you growth emerges from navigating these opposing forces. By acknowledging paradox rather than avoiding, you open the door to profound self-awareness and transformation. Remarkably, what at first *seems* like a dead-end becomes a portal into a new path.

The experience of Soul Paradox can be uncomfortable. You are challenged to confront the parts of self which feel uncertain, vulnerable, or conflicted. However, discomfort is not a signal to stop. Challenge is an invitation to explore. Paradox asks you to sit with the ambiguous, gray areas of life, where clarity is not immediate and must be cultivated through reflection, patience, and choice.

The Role of Fear in Soul Paradox

Fear is a natural part of the human experience and plays a significant role in fueling Soul Paradox. When you step toward your calling, fear arises as a protective mechanism, attempting to shield you from perceived risks or uncertainties. Recognizing this fear as a part of the process rather than a barrier, helps you approach life with curiosity and compassion.

While uncomfortable, fear is not inherently negative. Like a warning signal, fear alerts you to areas where growth and transformation are possible. Thus, instead of viewing fear as obstacle, consider its appearance as a companion on your journey. Fear is a guide pointing to the edges of your comfort zone, where meaningful change can occur.

Origins of Fear

As a tool of manipulation, fear *seems* to be unavoidable. As added pressure, common thought instructs you to eliminate fear as the primary response. Thus, when it appears, self-judgment kicks in and prompts a sense of personal failure.

However, no matter what you try, the reality is that fear will appear. The motion needed is not to pretend it's not there or push to eliminate it. In the face of fear, know you have choice in *how* you respond. When it appears, fear is guiding you toward choice and toward what no longer serves and is ready for release. Fear is showing where you have choice.

No matter where you are in your journey, there can be concern, worry, and fear which underlies your desires, dreams, and choices. Better to bring forward awareness of fear than to ignore or deny. Better to use fear as the path through turbulence.

Fear originates from a variety of sources. Plus, societal norms and expectations instill fears about stepping outside conventional paths. For instance, someone pursuing a creative career may worry about financial stability due to societal emphasis on traditional jobs. Similarly, societal definitions of success can amplify fear of judgment, making it difficult to pursue a calling deviating from the norm.

This is especially true when early childhood experience shapes beliefs about safety, success, and self-worth. A child raised in a risk-averse environment may grow into an adult who hesitates to take bold steps toward Soul Calling, carrying ingrained fears of failure or rejection.

Memories of previous disappointments can cast long shadows, amplifying the fear of failure. When you've faced setbacks before, it's easy to believe history will repeat itself, creating resistance to new opportunities.

Common Fears in Soul Paradox

Fear manifests as specific concerns and forms the tension within Soul Paradox. How fear manifests in your life is based on your experience, your choices, and the consequences of choice and experience. Common to many are these six forms of fear:

Fear of Not Being Good Enough: A deep-seated belief you are unworthy and, therefore, do not merit success or fulfillment. This fear undermines confidence and creates self-doubt, even in the face of clear opportunities.

Fear of Failure: Worrying you will not succeed or that your efforts will be wasted. This fear can lead to procrastination or avoidance, even when your calling feels deeply meaningful.

Fear of Judgment: Concern about how others will perceive you or your choices or actions. This fear keeps you from sharing your talents, speaking your truth, or stepping into the spotlight.

Fear of Change: Hesitation to step out of your comfort zone. Even when the current situation feels limiting, the familiarity provided can feel safer than the unknown or the uncertain.

Fear of Missing Out: The worry that by choosing one path, you are losing another. This fear can keep you in a state of indecision, endlessly evaluating options without committing to any of them.

Fear of Exposure: the worry of being truthfully you will open you to ridicule. Especially witnessing the defamation of others, you hold back, keep quiet, and change yourself.

Reframing Fear as a Tool for Growth

Fear is not insurmountable. By acknowledging your fear and exploring origins, you can begin to reframe fear as opportunity for growth. Fear contains valuable insights about what is important to you and where you feel vulnerable, making it a powerful tool for self-discovery.

Consider fear as a mirror reflecting your inner world. For example, the fear of failure might highlight a deep desire to succeed in a meaningful way. The fear of judgment might reveal a longing to be seen and accepted for who you truly are. Each fear holds a clue about your core needs and aspirations, providing a map for navigating Soul Paradox with greater clarity.

To reframe your fear from seeming obstacle to path of release and growth, consider these suggestions.

Begin by naming your fear. Fear pulls you into a future where you don't feel you have the power to deal with its present moment effects. When you shift your words from the future to the present – *I feel this fear now* – you bring your attention to this moment where you have the capacity to deal with the identified fear. Get specific as best you can. Notice *what if* especially in the form of a question. *What if I fail? What if I'm not good enough?* To name your fear and identify fear's flow in your awareness, pay attention to *what if*.

Next, trace fear's origin. Reflect on where the fear comes from. Fear has many sources including past experience, societal expectation, or inherited belief. Understanding its roots can help you separate the fear from your present reality.

Engage with curiosity. Instead of panic or more worry, be a like a fly on the wall, observing at arm's length. Ask questions like: *What is this fear trying to protect me from? What does my fear reveal about what matters most to me?* This practice shifts your perspective from avoidance to exploration.

Take small steps. As you look into your fear, reassure yourself you are not required to get rid of all fear forever. Instead take small steps. Break down your paradox into manageable actions. Each step forward, no matter how small, builds confidence and lessens the hold of fear.

Reframe fear as a signal for growth. Allow these steps to help you reframe the narrative of the fear. Instead of seeing fear as a sign to stop, see fear as a signal of growth. Remind yourself fear accompanies meaningful change, and its presence is a natural part of pursuing your Soul Calling.

Finally, release fear by questioning the premise. Simply ask: *Is this fear true?* More importantly is to question the validity of the fear as obstacle. *Will I allow this fear to hold me back?* When fear is named, you give yourself the opportunity of choice. You get to choose *how* you respond to the fear and explore *how* to release and move forward.

By engaging with fear rather than avoiding it, you transform fear from a barrier into a bridge from obstacle to opportunity. Fear becomes less about stopping you and more about pointing you toward the areas where you are most alive, vulnerable, and ready to grow. Embracing the role of fear in paradox allows you to move forward with courage and trust, deepening connection to your truth.

Tensions Within Explored

Remember, within paradox, the primary motion is to get beyond what *seems* at first to be an unconquerable obstacle. Thus, to explore the conflict on a deeper level, examine the inherent tension and then the clarity which comes from naming the fear.

For example, think on Sophia who dreams of starting her own artisanal bakery. Every morning, she wakes up envisioning the warmth of fresh bread, and the sound of laughter in her cozy café. Yet, the fear of failure whispers, *What if no one comes? What if I can't sustain it?* Coupled with that is the fear of not finishing – she worries she might start but run out of resources or energy before her dream becomes a reality. At first, these fears hold her back, even as her longing to create something meaningful grows stronger every day. She takes her worries seriously, and creates a strategy to help her move beyond, and confidently opens her bakery.

Ethan's heart pulls him toward the freedom of exploring the world, yet his fear of change and fear of not being enough keep him tethered to the security of his corporate job. *What if I can't handle the uncertainty? What if I lack the resilience to adapt to a nomadic lifestyle?* Adding to his hesitation is the fear of missing out – he worries that leaving his stable life might mean giving up future opportunities in his career. This tension leaves him torn between the craving for adventure and the security of the familiar. Yet, having named his concerns, he begins by taking short week trips to see what works and what other fears arise.

Maya yearns to share her art with the world. She desires to be seen. Yet, the fear of judgment looms large: *What if they don't understand my vision? What if they criticize my ability?* Compounding her struggle is the fear of not being enough – the nagging thought that her skills or ideas might fall short. This internal battle keeps her art hidden, even as her desire to connect through her creativity intensifies. Like Ethan, Maya acknowledges her concerns and begins by finding a small coffee shop excited to display her work.

Carlos is offered his dream job in a city teeming with opportunity. The prospect excites him because he feels an inner push to move forward. But, his fear of change whispers doubts: *What if I don't fit in? What if I lose my connection to my roots?* Adding to the conflict is his comfort of staying still – he worries that leaving might mean missing precious moments with friends and family. The paradox holds him in place, even as his calling urges him to take a bold step forward. Hearing his *what ifs*, he consults with several good friends and several family members about how to stay in touch when he sets out.

Jordan feels drawn to reconnect with others, yearning to build meaningful relationships. However, the fear of vulnerability and fear of judgment hold them back: *What if I open up and they reject me? What if they don't value what I bring to the table?* Overlaying this is the fear of not being enough – the belief that they lack the qualities needed to sustain deep connections. These fears create a cycle of withdrawal, even as their soul longs for closeness and community. In looking at the fear, Jordan realizes they were trying to solve all the fear all at once. Taking a step back, they decide to focus on one relationship at a time.

Embracing the Wiggle Room

A key aspect of working with Soul Paradox is embracing the *wiggle room*. Paradox is rarely black and white. Rather, paradox exists in gray areas where *seemingly* opposing truths coexist. For example, you can feel both excited and scared about pursuing your calling. You can believe in your potential while still doubting your abilities. Wiggle room is not a flaw in your process. Wiggle room offers a dynamic space where growth and discovery occur.

Imagine standing on a suspension bridge swaying gently in the wind. On one side lies your fear, whispering doubts and caution. On the other side stands your truth, calling you toward possibility and alignment. The swaying is the wiggle room where you learn to balance opposition finding strength in the tension. Neither eliminating fear nor rushing toward the truth, allow the sway to guide your steps as you move forward with awareness and courage.

Wiggle room appears when you let go of judging yourself for the appearance of fear in your life. Wiggle room also opens when you quit ignoring or when you no longer allow the fear to dictate reaction, withdrawal, or denial.

This wiggle room provides space to navigate the natural tension between fear and truth. Instead of trying to resolve paradox by choosing one side, you learn to hold both realities at once. For instance, you can acknowledge the fear of failure while also embracing the excitement of starting something new. You can accept the vulnerability of showing your work to the world while recognizing the deep satisfaction of self-expression. By holding what *seems* to be in opposition, you create the conditions for growth and resilience. You choose to not allow fear to hold you back, make do, or give up.

Learning to embrace wiggle room requires patience and self-compassion. It's not easy to sit with discomfort or to resist the urge to force clarity. However, within this space, you cultivate trust in yourself and the process. Each time you navigate paradox without rushing to resolution, you strengthen your ability to tolerate uncertainty and act truthfully despite the unknown. Here are several helpful questions:

Where is the wiggle room in this paradox?

What new perspective opens my awareness to expanded flexibility within this paradox?

How does the wiggle room strength self-trust?

Wiggle room is where your flexibility and creativity come alive. This is the opportunity where unexpected insights emerge, often revealing solutions or pathways which at first weren't immediately obvious. By allowing yourself to stay open and curious, you discover that the wiggle room is not just a place of tension but also a source of possibility. This awareness strengthens your ability to trust yourself and move forward despite uncertainty, transforming paradox from a stumbling block into a steppingstone for growth.

Identifying Soul Paradox

To find the related paradox of your calling, ask the related primary question:

> *What is the Soul Paradox of my Soul Calling?*

And just like Soul Calling, the response may come immediately or take a bit to bubble up.

Remember the paradox may be embedded in fear. Pay attention to the *what ifs*. Pay attention to assumptions or to the way you believe your Soul Calling is not possible. Pay attention to how you feel when you think on your Soul Calling. Feel into resistance, feel into any sense of *I can't*. Be courageous and look under the surface where you'd rather not look. Look at your discomfort, at your hesitation, at your denial

Imagine a series of fences between you and your Soul Vision. Walk up to the first fence and ask the fence to tell you why it's there and what fear, assumption, or belief is keeping you from moving forward. Decide if this is a limit you want to maintain, question its validity, name its origin. Be curious and be willing to let go.

Remember, small steps. Let go of self-judgment and seek assistance especially when the paradox *seems* insurmountable. Turn to the Soul Compass questions to poke at your unconsciousness and examine your resistance and discomfort. Just one deep breath can help you find the wiggle room and find your bridge and the confidence to cross from the seemingly slammed door to the newly open door.

Transforming Paradox into Growth

When you engage with Soul Paradox, blocks transform from a source of resistance into a catalyst for growth. By facing your fears, you not only move closer to your calling but also deepen your self-awareness and resilience. Each time you navigate paradox, you strengthen your ability to trust yourself and adapt to life's challenges.

Failure to address paradox is the primary reason efforts like new year's resolutions fail. Following purpose received from external authority fails for the same reason. While addressing paradox doesn't guarantee success, the courage to do so instills strength and resiliency into Soul Vision, expanding possibility and accomplishment.

Paradox holds this transformative power because it challenges you to expand your perspective and embrace ambiguity or complexity. The appearance of obstacle pushes you to confront your fears, question limiting beliefs, and reframe obstacles as opportunities. Through this process, paradox becomes a teacher, offering lessons to guide you toward greater alignment with your truth.

For example, someone who feels called to start a new career but fears failure might begin by taking a single class or exploring the new field part-time. Over time, small successes build confidence and reduce the hold of fear. This incremental growth illustrates how paradox can act as a bridge between where you are and where you want to be, illuminating the path forward with greater clarity and purpose.

Paradox also fosters creativity and innovation. When you hold space for seemingly opposing truths, you allow new possibilities to emerge. This creative tension leads to breakthroughs, both in how you understand yourself and how you navigate your calling. By embracing the discomfort of paradox, you unlock a deeper sense of empowerment and adaptability, enabling you to approach life with curiosity and confidence.

Deeply interconnected with Soul Calling and Soul Vision, Soul Paradox doesn't exist in isolation. Your calling inspires you to move forward, while paradox reveals the fears and doubts that must be addressed along the way. Vision provides the pathway for transforming clarity into action, helping you navigate the paradox with purpose and direction.

Again, this interaction creates a dynamic process of discovery, challenge, and fulfillment. By embracing your paradox, you unlock new possibilities for growth and alignment, bringing your calling into clearer focus and your vision into reality.

Navigating Soul Paradox in Real Life

Soul Paradox often presents itself as an inner tug-of-war, where fear and desire pull in opposite directions. At the heart of this tension lies the opportunity for profound growth and transformation.

Each paradox is unique, shaped by the unique feedback between personal fears and the deep call of the soul. The following stories illustrate how individuals can face their own paradoxes with courage and creativity, transforming moments of conflict into pathways toward alignment and fulfillment. The challenges of Soul Paradox are not barriers – they are invitations to embrace the complexity of personal truth.

For example, Anna, a dedicated high school teacher, always dreamed of becoming a writer but felt anchored by the stability of her teaching career. The fear of change weighed heavily on her. *What if I fail? What if I can't make a living as a writer?* Yet, her calling whispered persistently, nudging her to pick up her pen.

Anna started small, carving out quiet weekend mornings to pour her stories onto the page. With trembling hands, she submitted her first short story to a local magazine. To her surprise, it was published. Small victories accumulated, building her confidence. Eventually, Anna transitioned into a successful writing career. She often reflects on her journey, realizing her fear wasn't a barrier but a signal of the profound transformation possible on her life's path.

As a second example, Raj, a corporate professional, was deeply passionate about mental health advocacy but feared how his personal vulnerability would be perceived. The thought of sharing his struggles with anxiety in a corporate environment filled him with dread. *What if they think I'm weak? What if I damage my career?*

With courage sparked by his calling, Raj started small. He opened up to a trusted colleague about his experiences. Encouraged by the support he received, he began initiating conversations about mental health in team meetings. Step by step, he built momentum, eventually leading a company-wide initiative to foster mental health awareness. The response was overwhelmingly positive, with colleagues sharing how much his bravery inspired them and released them from embarrassment about their own challenges and dreams. Raj's journey demonstrates how stepping into vulnerability can pave the way for profound connection and change not just for one, but for many.

Emily, a software engineer, felt torn between the safety of her high-paying job and the magnetic pull of her dream to travel and document her adventures as a blogger. The fear of stepping away from financial stability was daunting. *What if I fail to make a living? What if this dream destroys my entire life?*

Emily found a middle ground by saving strategically and taking short trips while working remotely. With each journey, her blog gained followers, and her confidence grew. Her stories of adventure resonated deeply with her audience, eventually allowing her to transition to a full-time digital nomad lifestyle. Emily's journey taught her that the tension between security and freedom didn't require an all-or-nothing approach – it required realistic awareness of possibility to experience balance and trust in the process.

Next, consider Sofia, a volunteer coordinator at a local food bank. She felt a stirring within her to take on a larger leadership role in her organization. However, she couldn't shake the nagging doubts. *What if I'm not good enough? What if I let everyone down?* The weight of her self-doubt felt paralyzing, holding her back from the impact she longed to create.

Determined to honor her calling, Sofia sought out mentorship and enrolled in leadership training programs. These experiences became transformative, equipping her with both the skills and the confidence she needed. When the opportunity arose, she stepped into a leadership role, creating initiatives which brought lasting change to her community. Sofia's journey from doubt to leadership inspired others around her to rise into their own potential, proving that self-doubt can be a catalyst for growth when faced with courage and intention.

Liam, an entrepreneur with a passion for sustainable design, felt a deep calling to create eco-friendly furniture. However, his fear of failure loomed large. *What if no one buys it? What if I can't compete with bigger companies?* These doubts nearly kept him from starting.

However, Liam decided to take a small step. He created a prototype in his garage and shared it with close friends for feedback. Their encouragement fueled his confidence to refine his design and launch a Kickstarter campaign. At first the response was sluggish. Yet, he asked for feedback and shifted how he described his design. This shifted response and his campaign was fully funded. The initial setback helped him position his furniture, expand his offerings, and create a successful business. In this journey, Liam learned fear of failure doesn't mean stop. On the contrary, fear means proceed with clear intention and persistence, trusting the process of learning and growth.

Remember, successfully navigating Soul Paradox is not about eliminating fear or achieving instant clarity. Rather, the process of Soul Paradox is about finding balance in the tension, taking small but meaningful steps, and trusting the unfolding process. Fear may walk beside you, but it doesn't have to dominate or control. By embracing the exchange between fear and calling, you open the door to transformation, creating a life which reflects your deepest truth and powerful potential. Within this dance exists your powerful capacity to grow, evolve, and live within your Soul Calling.

The Bridge Between Soul Calling and Soul Vision

As already mentioned, Soul Paradox doesn't exist in isolation and is deeply interconnected with Soul Calling and Soul Vision. These three elements form the foundation of Soul Compass, creating a dynamic and synergistic framework for navigating life with clarity and purpose.

Soul Calling, as the voice of your inner truth, inspires you to move toward alignment with your deepest intentions and dreams. However, as you respond to your calling, Soul Paradox naturally arises to highlight the fears, doubts, and resistance challenging your progress. Paradox becomes the space where your calling is tested, asking you to confront and release the limiting beliefs holding you back.

Soul Vision bridges the gap between the clarity of your calling and the challenges revealed by paradox. While Soul Calling illuminates what resonates deeply, and Soul Paradox uncovers what stands in the way, Soul Vision provides the pathway for moving forward. Vision transforms the insights gained from engaging with paradox into actionable steps, enabling you to embody your truth and create a life aligned with your calling.

This interaction works in ongoing cycles. As you deepen your connection to your calling, new paradoxes may emerge, presenting fresh challenges and opportunities for growth. Each time you navigate this cycle, your vision evolves, reflecting a more deeply integrated version of yourself. For example, someone who feels called to pursue a creative career but struggles with self-doubt may initially focus on small projects to build confidence. Over time, their vision expands to include larger-scale initiatives, demonstrating how engaging with paradox refines and strengthens both their calling and their path forward.

This interconnected process highlights the importance of embracing paradox as a vital part of the journey. Rather than viewing resistance as a setback, you can experience a necessary step toward deeper understanding and alignment. The reciprocity of calling, paradox, and vision creates a holistic approach to personal and spiritual growth, enabling you to navigate life with resilience, curiosity, and connection.

Broader Spiritual Implications of Soul Paradox

Soul Paradox reflects a profound truth about the human experience: growth and transformation arise from tension and complexity. On a spiritual level, paradox invites you to transcend the polarized thinking of *either-or* and embrace a more expansive perspective.

The process of paradox asks you to hold space for seeming conflict – fear and courage, doubt and clarity, resistance and alignment – recognizing that these apparent opposites are not mutually exclusive but deeply interwoven. Instead of *either-or*, life is more a process of *either-and*.

This understanding aligns with the spiritual concept of unity beyond duality. By engaging with paradox, you tap into the interconnectedness of all things, where seemingly opposites coexist in balance and harmony. Paradox mirrors the natural rhythms of life, such as day and night, expansion and contraction, or creation and destruction, teaching you to honor the cyclical nature of existence.

Soul Paradox also deepens your relationship with the unknown – deepens your willingness to trust engagement with the unexpected. Spiritual growth involves stepping into mystery and trusting the unfolding process within the unknown – especially when the outcome is unclear. Paradox becomes a gateway to greater surrender and faith, encouraging you to let go of rigid expectations and allow your path to reveal itself organically, in the moment.

Productive people are trained to anticipate each and every step before beginning. However, by embracing the broader spiritual implications of paradox, you cultivate a deeper connection to yourself, with others, and within the larger flow of life. This perspective transforms paradox from a source of frustration into a sacred, revered teacher, guiding you toward wholeness, alignment, and empowerment.

Moving Forward with Courage

Engaging with Soul Paradox requires courage, curiosity, and a willingness to step into the unknown. This process asks you to trust your truth and believe in your ability to navigate uncertainty. While fear and doubt may not disappear entirely, they no longer hold you back. Instead, they become steppingstones on the path to greater alignment and purpose.

Remember, paradox is not a sign of failure or misalignment. It is an integral part of the journey, offering you the opportunity to grow and evolve. By embracing Soul Paradox, you unveil inner truth and create a life reflecting the fullness of who you are and can become.

Paradox is your soul's way of reminding you growth emerges from the space where fear and courage meet. Embrace this meeting, and let paradox guide you toward your truth in this moment as you move forward on life's path.

In this moment,

the Soul Paradox of my journey

shifts doubt into truth and

challenge into possibility.

10

SOUL VISION: CREATING THE PATH

**In this moment with trust,
I open to the vision of my truth.**

SOUL VISION IS THE PROCESS OF TRANSFORMING THE CLARITY OF YOUR Soul Calling and the lessons of your Soul Paradox into actionable steps.

Soul Vision is about envisioning a life aligned with your truth and crafting a path to bring your deepest intentions and dreams into reality. Soul Vision bridges the gap between inspiration and action, offering direction while leaving room for flexibility and evolution.

What is Soul Vision?

Soul Vision emerges when you tune into your inner truth and translate it into a vision for how you want to live, grow, and participate in the world. This vision is not a rigid blueprint but a dynamic and adaptive process evolving as you do. Unlike a destination-focused goal, Soul Vision emphasizes the journey itself – the continual process of alignment with your calling and the navigation of the paradox which arises along the way.

At its heart, Soul Vision is both practical and profound. It grounds the abstract elements of your calling and paradox into tangible actions, while also inspiring you to dream beyond what seems immediately possible. It calls you to imagine the life you most desire and invites you to take steps, however small, to create vision as reality.

Soul Vision is deeply personal and unique to each individual. For one person, it might involve building a creative career reflecting a passion for storytelling, while for another, vision means fostering rescue animals. The beauty of Soul Vision rests in its flexibility, adapting to your intentions, dreams, and circumstances while offering a guiding light to move forward.

This vision does not require perfection or certainty. Soul Vision thrives on clarity about what's important to you in this moment and your willingness to take action aligned with your truth. Soul Vision also leaves room for the unexpected, welcoming opportunities and shifts to enhance your path. By embracing this fluidity, you cultivate resilience and the determination to remain open to new possibility.

For example, through Soul Vision, a teacher might envision writing a book to transform how students engage with learning. A young professional may see their vision as creating a career that merges sustainability and innovation. While a parent might dream of fostering stronger connections within their family by modeling truth and courage.

Soul Vision combines inspiration with practicality, guiding you to craft a path reflecting the fullness of who you are and who you are becoming.

The Process of Building Soul Vision

Creating Soul Vision begins with this primary question:

What is the Soul Vision aligned with my Soul Calling?

You take steps to understand what you already know needs to be part of your vision. You look deeper into the intention of your calling. You make a list of what you feel is true or needed within your vision. You begin with what you feel and what you know already.

To deepen or expand your vision, ask more questions:

What does an aligned and authentic life look like for me?

Where will my calling take me?

How will I get to my Soul Calling?

How can I express my Soul Calling in practical ways?

To create my vision, what obstacles revealed by my Soul Paradox need to be addressed?

Thus, Soul Vision begins as a process of reflection, requiring thought, attention to feeling and intuitive awareness. Next is clarity which comes by leaning into uncertainty and the challenges which the awareness of calling and paradox has yet to resolve. Most importantly is openness to the ebb and flow which following Soul Vision will ignite. This means you know Soul Vision in this moment provides direction forward and what you eventually achieve may be very different than where you begin in this moment.

The broad, initial strokes of Soul Vision emerge through three perspectives:

What:

Emerging from Soul Calling, determining *what* is a process of beginning with the end in mind. Your calling creates an idea of where you're headed, pointing you in a direction toward the *what* of your vision.

Why:

Here you focus on what's important and *why*. This includes the values, priorities, and principles of your Soul Calling. In other words, the *why* is what gives meaning to calling.

How:

The steps, actions, or efforts which align with the *why* and get you to the *what*. This is the journey, the path, the process – *how* vision creates calling.

For some, getting to what, why, and how is relatively simple and straightforward. For example, if your calling in this moment is a summer vacation, The *what* is a summer vacation. The *why* can be to get a break you can afford in a place which touches your heart and brings joy. The *how* involves a bit of research in possibilities, conversation with friends, and then feeling into which possibility answers your calling. However, even within this simplicity, there is feedback happening which adjusts vision moment to moment. Comments from friends can clarify location and possible activities. More research can shift location again. What began as a possible beach trip to California in June turns into a hiking adventure to the Oregon Coast in July.

The point being that the process of defining vision begins in the moment and then ebbs and flows as you work out your intention, priority, and desire for the *what*, the *why*, and the *how*.

When Soul Calling is more dramatic or more impactful, then defining Soul Vision clearly from the very beginning isn't typical. You do as much as you can. You get as much clarity as you can, reflecting, thinking, feeling, researching. You do this until you get to the point of not knowing what else to do.

Then it comes to you – you will have the awareness that you've already begun your Soul Vision journey – you are already moving forward following Soul Calling. *What's my next step?* This is the question to ask, to find your way, to pivot toward clarity and understanding, to fully illuminate Soul Vision.

How to Define What, Why, and How

For *what*, write down a statement expressing your Soul Calling. Include everything you know and feel about your calling. For example, *I want to move* or *I want a new job* or *It's time for me to write a book*. At this point specifics are not required – yet include any specifics you already know. For example, *I want to move before August*, or *I want a new job in my current company*, or *It's time for me to write a book for children*.

To identify *why*, reflect on the principles or values that matter most to you especially in relation to your calling. Ask:

> *Why is this calling important to me now?*

Your Soul Vision will align with these values, ensuring your actions feel meaningful and true to your essential self.

Next, focus on what feels most significant in this moment. Identify priority or if you have a feeling of what comes first and what follows.

Feel into the intention embedded in your calling. Create clear, intention-driven statements capturing the essence of what you want to bring into your life. Examples include *I intend to cultivate creativity in my daily routine by setting aside time for writing*, or *I intend to build deeper connections by dedicating one evening a week to quality time with loved ones*.

To define the *how*, envision the ways your calling can come to life. Think expansively and remain open to unexpected opportunities. Brainstorm. Spend time visualizing what your ideal day or year might look like if you are aligned with your vision. Jot down or draw what comes to mind. Translate your reflections into a step-by-step plan. Include both short-term actions and long-term intentions.

Allow your imagination to open. Allow possibility to bloom in your awareness. This is the moment where your movie of your vision plays before you. Feel free to audition multiple scenarios. Often the vision is a collage of different scenes which fall into place bit by bit.

Awareness of possible *hows* will take you back to re-consider what and why. Your *what* can be refined and meaning becomes clearer and more nuanced. Back and forth, refining, re-defining, and envisioning the steps of *how* which express *what* and align with *why*.

No matter your Soul Calling, and no matter the process of creating Soul Vision, you will come to one of two points. In the first is you feel your soul Vision is clearly elaborated and you feel ready to follow the path of your vision.

In the second possibility, you have clarity about your calling and yet only parts of your vision. You have a general idea of where you're headed but probably not sure of exactly *how* to get there. You have a strong sense of *why* and your direction. You might be clear about the first step or two, but the path gets foggy thereafter.

The good news is the next movement is the same for either possibility. Now is the time to ask the fourth primary Soul Compass question:

What is my next step?

If you're ready to go, then your next step is *how* you begin, *how* you put Soul Vision into action. Make a roadmap with both short-term and long-term steps.

If you feel you lack clarity, then this question helps you make an important decision. Do you do more research or reflection in search of clarity? Or do you take a leap of faith and begin your journey trusting the fog will clear as you trust yourself and your steps forward will reveal more of the path and the *how* of your vision. Make a list of what you know in this moment and include what needs clarity and what questions need answers.

Either way, essentially, this is the point where possibility meets reality and you will respond based on self-trust and self-responsibility. Fundamentally you'll know when it's time to begin and when it's time to reconsider. Trust yourself.

Know at this point you can't make a mistake because the process of Soul Vision doesn't require perfection. Rather this is a process which supports a continual evolution of vision fed by experience and the inevitable feedback from each step you take.

This is why, especially within Soul Vision, when you get to a point where you don't see a way forward, through, or around – stop. Take a deep breath. Then, ask:

What is my next step?

These steps provide a structure for turning your inner truth into tangible action. However, remember that this process is dynamic and will require adjustments as you grow and encounter new experience.

Aligning Vision with Action

Soul Vision gains power when paired with action. Even the most expansive vision remains abstract until it is grounded in real-world steps. Begin by identifying the first small step you can take today. Action doesn't have to be perfect or grand; it simply needs to move you closer to alignment between calling and vision.

For example, if your calling involves creating art, your first step might be dedicating time to sketching or exploring a new medium. If your vision includes building stronger relationships, a first step could be reaching out to a loved one for a meaningful conversation. Or if your calling feels tied to a career change, your initial action might be researching opportunities or taking a single course in a new field.

Not just about moving forward, action is also a way of building confidence and self-trust. Each small step reinforces your connection to your truth and demonstrates that progress is possible, even in the face of fear or uncertainty. By taking just one step, you transform your vision from an abstract idea into living, breathing reality.

Persistence is key. Keep to small steps and break big efforts into smaller actions. Create an affirmation to align and remind yourself of the truth of your vision. Each step, each effort keeps your vision alive and evolving.

Celebrate progress, no matter how small. Acknowledge each milestone to reinforce your commitment to the path you are creating. This celebration helps you stay motivated and reminds you that every action, no matter how modest, contributes to the larger tapestry of your Soul Vision.

By grounding vision in action, you create momentum. Each step builds confidence and reinforces your connection to your truth, making it easier to navigate the uncertainties and paradoxes as they arise.

The Cyclical Nature of Soul Vision

Like Soul Calling and Soul Paradox, Soul Vision is neither linear nor static. As you act on choice and gain new experience, your vision shifts, and either expands or becomes more focused. This cyclical process reflects the dynamic nature of life, where clarity deepens over time, and opportunities emerge in unexpected ways.

Each step taken toward your vision creates a feedback loop. Actions produce results, insights, and unexpected challenges, which in turn refine your vision. For example, pursuing a creative project may reveal new skills or passions you hadn't considered, prompting you to expand your vision. Conversely, a challenge might illuminate a limitation or fear that, once addressed, brings greater alignment and clarity.

Embracing this recurrent, evolving nature allows you to stay flexible and responsive. Instead of clinging to a fixed idea of your vision, you remain open to evolution. This might mean adjusting your path as new callings emerge or refining your priorities as circumstances change. For instance, someone initially focused on individual goals may find that collaboration or community work becomes a more fulfilling expression of personal vision.

Trusting your process helps maintain inner alignment while honoring the unfolding journey. Returning to reconsider various aspects of vision is not a sign of failure but evidence of growth and adaptability. The return allows you to respond truthfully to life's shifts, ensuring your vision remains a living, evolving guide.

To fully engage with this process, set aside regular moments for reflection. Ask yourself questions such as:

What have I learned from recent experience?

How has my vision shifted or expanded?

What new opportunities or challenges have emerged?

These reflective questions keep you attuned to your inner truth while honoring the dynamic interweaving of vision, calling, and paradox.

Overcoming Challenges to Vision

As you create and live your Soul Vision, challenges will inevitably arise. These obstacles can feel daunting, but with intentional strategies and thoughtful Soul Compass questions, you can navigate through challenge and maintain alignment with your vision. Here are common challenges and practical approaches to overcoming them.

Self-Doubt:

Doubt arises at the edge of awareness making you feel unqualified and less than. Doubt is the sinking feeling in the pit of your stomach and leaves you questioning your ability to achieve your vision. The responsive strategy is to begin by focusing on incremental progress. Start with small, manageable steps to build confidence and see that you can make progress. Celebrate every small success as evidence of your capability. When doubt shows up, ask:

> *What would I choose if I didn't doubt myself?*

Fear of Failure:

Fear comes in on wisps and flutters, painting a picture of doom, or disappointment. Fear whispers that you are too-something-wrong to avoid failure. You worry that pursuing your vision will result in frustration or wasted effort and you are to blame. In the face of this fear of failure, ask:

> *What can I do knowing I can't fail?*

Then tackle the fear by reframing failure as feedback and as information about that which needs attention, adjustment, or release. View setbacks as opportunities to learn and refine your vision rather than as definitive roadblocks. Remind yourself that even *mistakes* bring valuable insights.

Perfectionism:

The ugly head of perfectionism pokes its demand for attention in the places where you feel challenged or incapable you believe your vision must be perfectly defined before you can begin. Instead, embrace imperfection and focus on progress over perfection. Remind yourself that action creates clarity and momentum. The first step doesn't demand perfection. The only requirement is that the step just needs to be taken. The journey of your vision begins with one step. Just one. When you realize the demand for perfectionism is getting in the way, ask:

Why do I act as if I'm less than?

Overwhelm:

Overwhelm creates an excuse to avoid both potential failure and potential success. Perfectionism becomes the way you keep safe and never need to deal with fear or overwhelm or doubt. Especially as you begin, all the things can feel daunting. Working to get the puzzle pieces to fit can be overwhelming and seem beyond your ability to cope. You feel paralyzed by the size or scope of your vision. There's too, too much all at once. In other words, tackle the fear in overwhelm and think through a possible strategy. Ask this two-part inquiry:

What's the worst thing that can happen if I fail?

If this worst thing happens, what can I do?

Once more, break your vision into smaller, actionable steps. Prioritize what feels most achievable and focus on one task at a time. Small actions accumulate into meaningful progress. And when you know you've got a plan if the worst happens, you know you can respond with confidence in any moment.

Procrastination:

One of the best ways to avoid failure is to put off until tomorrow – always tomorrow. Procrastination is delaying action on vision due to fear, distractions, or lack of motivation. Ask yourself:

What is the source of my procrastination?

Is my Soul Vision (or Soul Calling) what I really want in this moment?

Sometimes procrastination is trying to bring to your attention that you are no long in alignment with vision. If this is the case, pause. Do a check-in with calling, paradox, and vision to see what needs realignment. If you feel the calling of your vision, recommit. Create a schedule or accountability system. Set specific times to work on your vision and involve a trusted friend or mentor to check in on your progress. Treat your vision as a priority appointment with yourself.

Lack of Clarity:

At any point, your path can feel unfocused or cloudy. You feel unsure about what your vision looks like or what's next. Spend time reflecting on your calling, intentions, and priorities. Use visualization exercises to imagine the life you want to create and why this is important to you. A lack of clarity can be hiding a new understanding or a new direction. By examining closely, clarity emerges through exploration and action. Then ask yourself:

What is my next step?

External Pressures:

Family, friends, and society at large can all have very definite opinions about what you should and shouldn't be doing. Opinions at odds with your vision. Opinions which push especially at the doubt, fear, judgment, and overwhelm that's already on your radar. Ask yourself:

Is there anything useful for me in the opinion of others?

Keep you and your vision as your focus and priority. Incorporate the helpful bits and let the rest go. Reconnect with your intention and priorities. Practice saying *NO* to demands not aligned with your truth. Seek out supportive communities or mentors who encourage your vision and understand your journey.

Fear of Uncertainty:

Each and every step of your life is into the unknown. Even though you seek guarantee and may feel you are certain about the future, the unexpected is a natural part of life. The unexpected will appear no matter how much you plot or ignore.

To stay away from the ignorance-is-bliss mode, look fear in the face. Seek to understand. Ask:

In this moment, what is my fear of the unknown?

This is you embracing uncertainty as part of the journey. Focus on taking one intentional action at a time and trust that clarity will emerge through the process. Reframe uncertainty as a space of possibility rather than limitation.

Limited Resources:

Feeling a sense of limitation, whether a lack of time, money, or support, is a frequent experience when you work toward your Soul Vision. The feeling of limitation can be a symptom of another concern, worry, or fear. Ask:

What is the fear hidden behind what seems to be a limitation?

Focus on what is within your control. Seek creative solutions and dedicate small pockets of time to your vision. Progress doesn't require perfection – it only requires persistence to take one more step.

Critical Voice:

The negative self-talk of your inner critical voice is discouraging and can undermine your progress. This snarky voice will show up especially in moments of challenge and doubt, spewing words which threaten and batter belief and vision. Here's the question to ask:

Are the words of my critical voice really true?

This question helps you to be mindful of your inner dialogue. Then replace negative thoughts with empowering affirmations, such as, *I am capable of creating a life aligned with my truth*. Speak to yourself with the kindness and encouragement you would offer a close friend.

OVERCOMING CHALLENGES TO YOUR SOUL VISION IS NOT ABOUT eliminating obstacles – it's about learning to move through them with courage, creativity, and grace. Each challenge is an opportunity to grow stronger, deepen your connection to your truth, and refine your path forward. Far from being signs of failure, these moments invite you to build resilience and embrace the evolving nature of your vision.

Challenges serve as milestones on your journey, offering chances to pause, reflect, and adjust. Reframing challenges as steppingstones rather than barriers. This transforms the process of bringing your vision to life into an ongoing dance of discovery and alignment.

Remember, vision isn't about perfection. Soul Vision only needs to be truthful *for you*.

The tools you use to navigate these challenges are more than strategies; they are steadfast companions, empowering you to face uncertainties with confidence and creativity. With each small step forward, you cultivate the clarity and strength to continue your journey. Trust yourself, trust the process, and know every action, no matter how small, is a celebration of your courage and commitment to living your truth.

The Positive Role of Intuition

Intuition plays a vital role in shaping and sustaining your Soul Vision. It is the quiet, inner voice – your voice of truth – guiding you especially when logic or external advice falls short. By tapping into your intuition, you connect with a deeper sense of knowing reflecting your truth and your vision.

Intuition allows you to perceive possibilities and opportunities that are not immediately obvious. Following intuition invites you to trust instinct when making decisions, even in the absence of complete information. For example, you might feel a strong pull toward a project or path that initially *seemed* unrelated to your current goals, only to discover later how strongly it aligns with your calling.

Listening to your intuition also fosters creativity and flexibility. Intuition helps you adapt your vision as new insights emerge, ensuring your path remains dynamic and responsive. When fear or doubt arise, intuition can serve as a grounding force, reminding you of the resonance and clarity that inspiring your vision in the first place.

To cultivate your intuition, create moments of stillness in your daily life to connect with the stillness in body, mind, heart, and soul. Journaling, meditation, Akashic Records practice, and spending time in nature are powerful tools for strengthening your connection to your inner guidance. By honoring your intuition, you enhance your ability to make choices which feel authentic and aligned with your Soul Vision.

Bringing Soul Vision to Life

Soul Vision is the bridge between your calling and the actions bringing calling to life. Soul Vision translates the whispers of your truth into tangible steps, creating a life aligned with your intentions and passions.

There are many paths which highlight the diverse ways individuals have embraced their Soul Vision, transforming dreams into reality. Vision isn't limited to grand gestures – it's rooted in small, intentional actions rippling outward, creating impact, feedback, and meaning.

Anna, a chef, felt a deep calling to address food insecurity in her city. This pull stirred both excitement and uncertainty. *How can one person make a difference?* She began by organizing weekly cooking classes for underserved families, teaching them how to prepare healthy meals on a budget. The joy in the children's laughter and the gratitude in their parents' eyes fueled her determination. Over time, Anna's vision expanded into a nonprofit organization providing meals, resources, and education for the community. What started as a small initiative became a beacon of hope, reminding her that even the smallest step aligned with passion can grow into something extraordinary.

Anna learned: *Starting small and aligning with personal truth can lead to larger, broader actions.*

David, a corporate lawyer, felt a growing disconnection from his work. While his career offered financial security, it lacked the personal fulfillment he craved. His passion for environmental activism called to him, though fear of change held him back. David began volunteering for local environmental nonprofits on weekends, using his legal expertise to support their missions. The satisfaction he felt during these moments ignited a vision of transitioning into a career aligned with this new calling. Over time, David shifted into a full-time role as a legal advocate for climate initiatives, finding a deep sense of purpose in his work.

David learned: *Aligning professional goals with personal truth creates fulfillment and purpose.*

Maria, a high school teacher, had always been drawn to storytelling but doubted her ability to write a novel. Her vision felt both thrilling and overwhelming – *Could she really make time for this while teaching full-time?* Determined to honor her calling, Maria committed to writing for 30 minutes each morning before work. The quiet hours became her sanctuary, a space where her creativity flourished. After a year of dedication, she finished her novel, which not only fulfilled her dream but inspired her students and community to pursue their own creative passions.

Maria learned: *Consistent small steps can transform a vision into reality, even alongside other responsibilities.*

Sofia realized her Soul Vision centered on strengthening family bonds. Growing up in a fragmented family, she longed to create a sense of unity for her loved ones. Her vision started with small gatherings – Sunday dinners filled with laughter and shared stories. Over time, she began hosting monthly family gatherings, initiating meaningful conversations that deepened connections across generations. These gatherings became a cherished tradition, and Sofia's vision sparked a ripple effect, inspiring younger family members to continue fostering these bonds.

Sofia learned: *Vision can focus on improving relationships and fostering connection rather than external achievements.*

Ron, an avid hiker, felt called to integrate mental health awareness into the running community. He had experienced firsthand how hiking helped him navigate his own mental health challenges and wanted to share this connection with others. He began by organizing small group hikes focused on mindfulness and emotional well-being.

The initial response was modest but heartfelt, encouraging Ron to expand his vision. Over time, his initiative grew into a regional network of events and workshops, helping others use hiking as a tool for mental health advocacy. Ron's vision transformed his personal passion into a platform for public service, creating a meaningful impact within his community.

Ron learned: *Personal passions can evolve into meaningful contributions to a broader community.*

While deeply personal, Soul Vision can also be profoundly impactful. Whether focused on transforming careers, nurturing relationships, or addressing community needs, each vision reflects the individual's truth. The common thread is the courage to take intentional steps forward, even in the face of uncertainty. Trust your vision, knowing that every action you take brings you closer to a life aligned with your soul's deepest calling. Your vision, no matter how small it seems, has the power to create ripples of transformation extending far beyond yourself.

Connecting Vision with Calling and Paradox

As already noted, Soul Vision is intricately connected to both Soul Calling and Soul Paradox. While calling illuminates your inner truth and paradox reveals the fears and challenges you must navigate, vision provides the path forward. It integrates the inspiration of your calling with the lessons of your paradox, transforming insight into action.

This exchange creates a powerful cycle of growth. Soul Calling inspires you to reach for alignment with your truth, while Soul Paradox invites you to confront the fears and doubts that arise along the way. Together, they provide the foundation for vision to take form. Soul Vision becomes the vehicle integrating the inner clarity of calling with the outer realities shaped by paradox, creating a dynamic process of reflection, action, and refinement.

Moreover, vision is not static. Soul Vision evolves in response to the deepening of calling and the resolution of paradox. As you act, new layers of your calling emerge, revealing fresh opportunities for growth. Similarly, the lessons learned from navigating paradox can expand the scope and depth of your vision, making it richer and more aligned with your essential self.

This ongoing interaction highlights the importance of flexibility and trust. Recognize that calling, paradox, and vision are not isolated elements but interconnected motions working together to guide your journey. By embracing their interaction, you create a life which reflects the fullness of who you are and honors your dynamic path of growth, transformation, and alignment.

Living Your Soul Vision

Living your Soul Vision is an ongoing practice of intention, action, and reflection. A practice which asks you to stay connected to your truth while remaining adaptable to life's changes. This is not about achieving perfection but about continually choosing alignment with your truth and calling.

Living your vision requires courage and persistence, especially in the face of challenges and uncertainty. You will acknowledge and navigate moments when progress feels slow or doubts creep in. These are the moments when recommitting to your truth and vision becomes most important.

To live your Soul Vision, take small, consistent actions to build momentum over time. Begin each day with a simple question:

To align with my Soul Vision today, what is my next step?

Reflect on the steps you've taken and the lessons learned along the way. Grateful awareness reinforces your progress and nurtures a positive mindset.

Flexibility helps you recognize when your vision shifts. This openness to change assists in analyzing the shift as new opportunity or new challenge. Be willing to adapt while staying true to your core values.

As within any motion of life, acknowledge your achievements, no matter how small. Celebrating progress fosters motivation and reinforces your commitment. Be sure to set time to evaluate your progress and recalibrate your actions. Reflection helps you stay aligned with your evolving vision.

Let your Soul Vision inspire you to dream boldly and act courageously. Trust each step you take, no matter how small, brings you closer to a life reflecting the fullness of who you are. By embracing the dynamic and evolving nature of your vision, you create a path honoring your truth and empowering you to live with purpose and possibility.

Living your Soul Vision is not a one-time achievement but a joyful, lifelong journey. This is a process which asks you to continually deepen your connection to your calling, refine your actions, and remain open to the unfolding possibilities include new calling, new paradox, and new vision. By approaching each day with intention and flexibility, you bring your Soul Vision to life in ways that are both practical and transformative.

An Invitation to Journey

Your Soul Vision is a gift, a reflection of your unique expression and the light you bring into the world. Vision responds to your call to engage with life in ways which feel deeply aligned and truthful. As you step into this journey, remember perfection is not required, and no step is too small. Each moment of intention and action contributes to the creation of a life resonating with your truth.

Take this as your call to action: commit to one meaningful step today. Whether it's reflecting on challenge, setting an intention, or taking a small action aligned with your vision, let today be the beginning of your next chapter. Trust your path will reveal itself as you walk. Know every step is guided by your inner truth and courage.

Your Soul Vision is waiting to unfold. Begin now, and let the journey inspire and transform you in ways you cannot yet imagine. The world is ready for the unique vision only you can bring.

Remember, your Soul Vision is a living expression of your truth. Every step you take toward it – no matter how small – creates a ripple of alignment and possibility.

Begin by asking now:

What is my next step?

In this moment,

I embrace the

infinite possibility

of my Soul Vision.

11

LIFE AS A SPIRAL PATH

In this moment,
I embrace the turns of my path.

THE PATH OF LIFE IS RARELY A STRAIGHT LINE. INSTEAD, THINK OF LIFE as a spiral path – a spiral where the cycles of experience, lesson, and growth return in new forms, offering expanded opportunities for deeper understanding and alignment.

Life as a spiral path is based on the energetic concept of the Eternal Return – meaning everything which flows out, returns. This is the inherent, energetic ebb and flow of life – a flow from the divine to human experience which returns always to the sacred.

Soul Compass, as a spiral path within the energetics of the Eternal Return, is an invitation to see life not as a series of destination points but as a restorative, ongoing journey of discovery, refinement, and renewal. By embracing the spiral nature of life, you can navigate the unknown and unexpected with greater trust and resilience.

Understanding the Spiral Path

The spiral path reflects the dynamic and cyclical nature of life. Each turn of the spiral revisits themes and challenges – and from a new perspective. What once seemed overwhelming may now appear manageable, and lessons that felt incomplete now reveal new insights.

The spiral reminds you that growth is not linear. Instead, personal growth is an evolving and revolving process of expansion and integration. Each cycle of the spiral brings you closer to your truth, allowing you to refine your understanding of your Soul Calling, confront your Soul Paradox, and expand your Soul Vision.

The Feedback Loop of Life

The Eternal Return operates as a feedback loop, where action, choice, and experience flow back to you, providing valuable insight for continued growth and expansion. This loop encourages you to reflect on what feels aligned and what needs adjustment, creating a continuous process of learning, transformation, and integration.

Each action you take creates an outcome, and that outcome, whether it feels like success or setback, is a source of information and intuitive understanding. For example, pursuing a creative project leads to unexpected collaborations, showing you new directions for your vision. Facing challenges in a relationship highlights areas where you need to set boundaries or communicate more effectively. Or revisiting an abandoned goal reveals untapped skills or passions aligned with your calling.

The feedback loop isn't just about identifying what works; it's also about acknowledging what doesn't. Setbacks and missteps are valuable teachers, offering clarity on where you need to refine your approach. Engaging with this continuous loop requires curiosity and compassion, allowing you to explore the *why* behind outcomes without judgment.

To actively engage with the feedback loop, look to your awareness, your intuition, your thoughts and feelings. Ask yourself reflection questions and write about your actions and choices, and their results:

Which actions or choices I am making are effective?

What actions or choices feel misaligned?

What insights do I gain from my actions and choices?

Pay attention to what arises in your awareness. Be mindful, observe. Contemplate the patterns in your life. Identify recurring themes or lessons. Contemplate how these inform your next steps.

Balance moments of solitude with community participation. Seek input from trusted friends or mentors who can offer an outside perspective on your journey.

Build cycles into your habits and schedule. Use the insights of reflection to refine your path and create a process which adds to and benefits from the spirals of your path. Adjust your actions, priorities, or vision as needed.

Dynamic and ever evolving, the feedback loop of life is not a linear process. Each turn of the spiral deepens understanding of your Soul Calling, strengthens your ability to navigate Soul Paradox, and expands your Soul Vision. By embracing this process, you cultivate resilience and adaptability, ensuring each cycle of growth brings you closer to living in alignment with your truth.

Navigating Your Spiral Path with Soul Compass

Not a passive process, the journey on your spiral path requires active engagement with your Soul Compass. Your active attention to your process brings awareness of the turns and returns on your path. Guided by the Eternal Return, your Soul Compass helps you navigate the spiral path of life with intention and connection.

Within Soul Calling, each turn of the spiral invites you to reconnect with your calling by asking:

What is my truth in this moment?

As you revisit recurring themes, your calling evolves, reflecting new insights, shifting priorities, or new layers of understanding. New calling within the various aspects of life will emerge asking to be included in your life. You will develop multiple callings across your life. The Eternal Return ensures your calling remains aligned with who you are becoming.

On your journey, Soul Paradox is your teacher. Paradox emerging within your spiral path highlights unresolved fears or limiting beliefs. Each time you confront paradox, you strengthen your capacity for courage and clarity. Each appearance is new opportunity to gain new understanding. Instead of a habit of limitation and as a teacher, paradox guides you toward greater clarity and courage. Ask:

Within this new perspective of paradox, what can I understand about my life?

Then, Soul Vision is your guide forward and provides a structure for refining your vision. As you integrate lessons from each return of the spiral, your vision expands and adapts. Vision becomes more nuanced, reflecting the depth of your growth and the possibilities emerging on your path. Vision becomes the guiding light that transforms insights into action, creating a dynamic cycle of discovery, growth, and alignment. You begin to apply this process of vision to the broad arc of your life and all the small and large projects which are your life. Ask:

Within the new expansion of my vision, what are the new possibilities in my life?

This interconnectedness reminds you that the Eternal Return is not merely a repetition of past patterns but an invitation to engage in new and transformative ways. Through the alignment of your Soul Compass, you can navigate the spiral path with confidence, trusting that each return offers fresh opportunities for growth and alignment.

Embracing Cycles of Rest and Action

Your spiral path includes natural cycles of rest and action, reflection and movement. These rhythms are essential for sustainable growth. Rest allows you to integrate what you've learned, while action propels you forward, putting your insights into practice.

Rest is not a sign of inactivity or weakness. Rest is a sacred opportunity for integration and renewal. During rest, your mind and body process the lessons from recent experiences, creating space for clarity and new perspectives to emerge. Rest can take many forms, such as mindful stillness, creative play, or simply allowing yourself time to recharge without guilt. Even just turning your head to look out a window or gaze in a new direction provides rest and opens the door for a new, shifted perspective. Embracing rest ensures that you avoid burnout and remain connected to your calling.

Action is where your insights take shape in the world. Action transforms the inner work of reflection into tangible steps bringing your vision to life. Action requires courage, persistence, and the willingness to embrace imperfection. Even small, consistent actions build momentum and reinforce your alignment with your truth.

The flow between rest and action creates harmony within. Too much rest without action can lead to stagnation, while excessive action without rest can result in burnout. To find balance, ask yourself:

What does my body, mind, and soul need right now?

Am I integrating what I've learned, or am I rushing forward without reflection?

Am I taking steps aligned with my truth, or am I acting out of habit or external pressure?

To find balance between rest and action, take intentional time for a break, time to reflect, time to step away from action. Schedule this and don't no-show yourself. With intention for rest defined, the action will become more intentional and more realistic.

Incorporate short moments of stillness into your daily routine. Make a habit of a short pause with eyes closed and a deep breath. Gaze out a window and let the energy of the day slow into the moment. These pauses help you stay connected to your truth. Acknowledge the progress you've made through both rest and action. Acknowledge accomplishment to reinforce the balance you've cultivated.

By honoring the cycles of rest and action, you align with the natural rhythms of life. This balance empowers you to navigate your spiral path with resilience, ensuring each turn brings you closer to your calling and vision.

Remember this: by trusting that periods of stillness are not stagnation but preparation for the next turn of the spiral, you create the opening to embrace powerful action. The rest helps you know when the time for bold steps toward your vision appear. In each moment, ebb and flow supports Soul Vision.

The cyclical nature of life is reflected in the natural ebb and flow of the natural world. From the changing seasons to the phases of the moon, nature reflects the spiral path in its rhythms of growth, decay, and renewal. By embracing this perspective, you align with the flow of life and deepen your connection to the greater whole.

Additionally, many spiritual traditions use the spiral as a metaphor for life's journey. Unlike a circle, which repeats without change, a spiral revisits themes from an expanded perspective each time. This perspective teaches that returning to familiar challenges or experiences is not regression but an opportunity to deepen your understanding and integration.

The Eternal Return also reflects the spiritual principle of unity within duality. Just as the spiral encompasses both movement outward and inward, your journey integrates opposites – light and shadow, joy and sorrow, action and rest. Recognizing and embracing these dualities allows you to move through life with greater harmony and acceptance.

Spiritual growth is a dance with the unknown. The Eternal Return invites you to trust the process of transformation, even when the path forward is unclear. By embracing each cycle as part of your unfolding journey, you cultivate faith in your ability to pilot the complexities of life.

Your personal spiral of growth is interconnected with the larger spirals of collective evolution. As you learn, heal, and align with your truth, the wake of your spiral expands possibility for all. This perspective reinforces the sacredness of your individual journey. Your spiral path is interconnected with the sacred nature of All That Is.

Seeing your journey as a spiral also invites you to approach life with awe-filled curiosity. Each return offers a new chance to grow, reminding you that perfection is not the goal – alignment, trust, and truth are the essence of your calling.

Real-Life Reflections of the Spiral Path

Guided by the eternal ebb and flow, your life's journey moves in spirals, revisiting themes, passions, and lessons with new layers of understanding. Thus, what was once set aside or a path which felt closed can reappear with a chance to engage in profound and transformative ways. Each return brings an invitation to reflect, grow, and integrate the wisdom of the past into the person you are becoming.

Susan had given up piano lessons in her teenage years, dismissing them as a childhood pastime. Decades later, after a demanding period in her career, she felt drawn to the piano once more. Initially, she played for personal joy, but as her relationship with the instrument deepened, it became a form of meditation and creativity. What began as a nostalgic return transformed into a spiritual cornerstone, offering her a sense of peace and alignment.

Know that the skills or passions you leave behind often reappear when you are ready to engage with them in deeper, more meaningful ways.

Alex had always dreamed of being an astronaut as a child but followed a more practical path into engineering. Years later, their company began collaborating on a space exploration project, reigniting their childhood wonder. Although they never became an astronaut, they contributed to space exploration in ways they had never anticipated, bringing their dream full circle.

Within your spiral path, dreams may not unfold as expected but can resurface in forms aligned with your current path.

Monica realized she was encountering the same relationship challenges repeatedly. When an old friend re-entered her life, she chose to approach the dynamic differently. This time, she sought support, set firm boundaries, and prioritized her emotional well-being. As a result, the friendship flourished into a healthier and more supportive connection, reflecting her inner growth.

Remember that returning challenges provide opportunities to respond with greater self-awareness and emotional resilience.

After moving abroad, Priya felt disconnected from her cultural roots and the rich traditions of her family. Years later, during a reunion, she found herself drawn to the elders' storytelling and traditional cooking. Relearning these practices became a way for her to honor her past while weaving them into her present identity, creating a sense of belonging and continuity.

From this situation, you can learn that returning to cultural roots can offer a sense of grounding and belonging, especially during life transitions.

Christine had casually practiced yoga during college, treating it as a fitness routine. Years later, facing burnout, she returned to yoga with fresh eyes, discovering it as a spiritual practice aligning body, mind, heart, and soul. This reconnection became a vital tool for navigating stress and fostering self-awareness, connecting Christine in a more holistic sense of well-being.

Soul Compass is at its heart a spiritual practice which can enter your life when you are ready to embrace your deeper expression.

Keep in mind: each time a skill, dream, challenge, tradition, or practice returns, it comes with a chance to engage with it from a place of deeper wisdom and understanding. Life's spirals are not redundant but essential, offering the chance to heal, evolve, and integrate all the threads of your journey. Trust the moments of return as signposts guiding you toward deeper alignment with your essential self.

Trust Your Spiral Path

Every turn of the spiral brings you closer to the essence of your truth, offering moments to realign, refine, and renew your path. By engaging with this dynamic process, you embrace life as an evolving journey rather than a series of fixed outcomes.

Take time to reflect on your current place within your spiral. Make a difference between revisiting a familiar challenge or stepping into a new opportunity. Pay attention to the lessons re-emerging and meet them with curiosity and compassion. Trust each cycle to equip you with the wisdom, resilience, and insight needed to move forward with a stronger connection to personal truth.

Engage with your spiral path by anchoring yourself in the present moment. Find ways to explore the cycles in your life. Celebrate how far you've come and acknowledge the courage it takes to embrace what lies ahead. Each step you take is a testament to your ability to grow and adapt, weaving your truth into the larger tapestry of your life.

Remember, your spiral path is not about perfection but about progress. Honor your journey, trusting that even the smallest step leads to profound transformation.

Allow the Eternal Return to be your guide, reminding you that growth is a process, not a destination.

Know that with each turn of the spiral, you align more deeply with your Soul Compass and live the life of your calling and your vision.

Within my spiral path,

everything I need moves toward me

quickly, easily, and safely.

12

IS THIS WHERE YOU STOP?

*In this moment,
I am connected
to my inner truth.*

THERE IS A FIFTH QUESTION FOR SOUL COMPASS. AN IMPLIED QUESTION, often asked in frustration or sometimes in despair. Yet, also, a question of truth and commitment.

Is this where I stop?

A valid question during many moments of the Soul Compass process. Yet one which requires courage to face because there *seems* to be an assumption of failure.

At first glance, the implication of this question is that there is only one reason to stop. You failed. You failed to hear your calling correctly.

You failed to navigate the contradictions of paradox perfectly. You failed to go beyond *seems*. You failed your vision and you failed yourself because you ... failed. And taken this way, stop and bring yourself into your own presence, and ask:

Is it my truth I've failed?

Yet, like so much in life, this question is not limited only to the surface of life. When you go beyond its initial appearance, when you take a breath and keep yourself from the precipice of blind reaction, beautiful layers are revealed.

In the unfolding you see this as a question for personal truth. A question to help you discern where you are with yourself and your life in this moment. This is a question revealing personal commitment.

Sometimes the reality of life is that you need a break, a moment to collect yourself. A moment to ponder. A moment to not think, not reflect, not push. You require rest, a stop, a deep breath.

Thus, in asking in this moment, your answer to the question may be simple. I don't know yet. I need a break. I need to give myself a moment to discern if this moment is one in which I stop my Soul Compass process – if I halt my vision and look elsewhere for my calling. At some point, life with only flow and no ebb will falter.

Rest is necessary to restore. Relaxation can stop the push – or at least slow the relentless motion. You need time to breathe, to let go, to enjoy the beautiful flow of your life. A moment to perch and allow the flow to just be while the ebb has its moment. Thus, not a full stop – a moment to collect yourself.

As you consider a response, you've given yourself a chance to consider the truth of you in this moment. A moment which can be filled with everything and nothing – hopefully without judgment, expectation, or demand. A moment of presence to observe and witness your ebb and flow within your calling, paradox, and vision.

As you work with your Soul Compass, frustration, confusion, disappointment can all indicate your truth is shifting. Awareness is asking for attention and, perhaps, shift or change.

If you are struggling with calling, the question – *Is this where I stop?* – refocuses your attention, shifts awareness, and may pivot direction. When you focus on you and what is truth for you in the moment, if you're calling has drastically changed, in this pause you give yourself an open window to reconsider.

Not all calling is to be seen to conclusion. Sometimes the truth of calling arises, and its conclusion is in its release or within integration with another calling.

The question of stopping can also cast a brighter light on challenge and contradiction. Maybe more paradox is pushing to the surface. The only way to be aware is to stop here, now, and look outside of self to receive from your depths within. Again, *seemingly* contradictory for in this moment of contemplation often the way to assess your inward journey is to look beyond self. To take a moment for life to be reflected back to you to gain clarity.

This is the gift of the pause. Between breath in and breath out is the dynamic gift of your connection with the infinite and eternal. The stillness of the all and nothing whispers, and you receive your fullness. Your essential self reverberates with the resonance of your spiral path.

THEN THERE ARE THOSE MOMENTS WHEN YOU ARE PUSHING HARD AND fast and this sustained effort is what brings vision to life. Clearly there is no need to stop or change course. All is in alignment. Calling and vision are united. Your spiral path beckons, and you feel resonance with the direction of your compass.

Then there are other moments where the demand and the expectation has you ramming ahead without alignment. You are bumping around in the dark unable to flip the switch of clear awareness. You are distracted, annoyed, dismayed. The more you push, the worse your disconnection from inner truth and integrity.

This is a moment when it takes an incredible gulp of courage to stop, to breathe, to deal with the panic, and to unravel worry at the root of the push. This is also a moment to set aside denial and arrogance. Time to clear the decks and acknowledge clearly your reality, your truth, and your commitment to your calling.

The reality of your Soul Compass process is that at any moment, your truth may be that you need to stop and acknowledge that it is time to change course. It's time to release your vision and your calling. Time to release for one simple, yet hard to admit reason. The paradox in the moment is that neither current calling nor current vision are aligned with your truth now.

You've grown, expanded, moved on. You've shifted and you are not the person you were. And because of these changes, your trajectory needs redirection and recalibration.

It's time to pivot toward a new awareness of truth, a new motion with a new intention. However difficult it is to admit it out loud, you feel the answer in your bones. Though your mind may struggle, your heart is aware. Yes, you say to yourself, it's time to stop. It's time to chart a new path. You feel the truth throughout your entire being.

There is relief. Tension falls. The push subsides. You feel alignment with your choice. You breathe deeply. Your ebb returns.

Most importantly, you make this choice not because you failed. You make this choice because you know, in this moment, this is your truth. This is a moment which can feel like an end to all ends. However, truth and integrity support your courage to do now what at another moment *seemed* unthinkable. And which, in this moment, is revealed, from the unknown, as deeply resilient personal truth.

Thus, the question:

Is this where I stop?

Now this is also a question of personal commitment. As you consider, the question is an opportunity to assess your life and your journey. In the pause, you feel into where you are. You check in with your calling. You check in with your vision. You feel into your essential self. You check the calibration of your willingness and commitment to the current path of your compass.

However fraught your journey may be, you can feel the threads of joy and excitement which initially stirred you to continue. You can feel the thrill of alignment into the cells of your soul. You may not be any clearer about the exact steps of your path than when you began. However, you know, you feel, you sense, you understand this *is* your life, your choice, your responsibility, your path.

No matter the paradox, you embody your commitment. You are willing to continue to forge your path in service of *your* vision. Calling and vision are aligned within you, and you are clear about your journey.

Then the question comes into deepest focus:

Is this where I stop?

No, you say.

I'll go on.

I will continue.

My truth in this moment is my commitment to myself within my spiral path. While there may be a moment to come when the truthful answer is otherwise, in this moment, this is not my inflection point.

This is a moment to speak my truth and choose my path accordingly.

In this moment, I will not stop.

In this moment, I feel into my Soul Compass and ask:

What is my next step?

In this moment,

my Soul Compass guides me

to follow the call of my soul, resolve paradox, and

thrive within aligned Soul Vision!

READY TO LEARN MORE?

You have been on a journey and I am honored to share it with you!

Life is full of the depth of challenge and opportunity. Full of what we can imagine and all that is beyond imagination.

If you'd like to find support in exploring the nuances and depth of your Soul Compass, I provide Akashic Record Readings which provide direction however you'd like to explore. In these sessions I am able to help you through the process, identify blocks and unseen aspects of paradox. Plus, I am particularly adept at the vision creating part!

If you'd like to go beyond the surface within your spiritual exploration, I have created *SpiritualDeepDive.com*.

And if you are ready to learn to access the Akashic Records, then check out my powerfully comprehensive and advanced program, *Akashic Records Intensive*. Plus *AkashicRecordInsights.com* has information, workbooks, and workshops to support your journey.

May you find the power of your Soul Calling, know your capacity within to transform your Soul Paradox so that life if full of the awesomeness of your Soul Vision!

Find everything at **CherylMarlene.com**.

BELIEVE. Laugh. Learn. Love. Be. Become. Always.

In Joy!

Cheryl

ABOUT CHERYL

www.CherylMarlene.com

Cheryl Marlene is a pioneering guide in spiritual consciousness and the Akashic Records, blazing a new path for seekers ready to move beyond superficial answers. Her work is for those who desire unvarnished truth, deep transformation, and a profound connection to personal power.

A mystic, futurist, and trailblazer, Cheryl expands the Akashic Records beyond outdated myths into a living, dynamic spiritual practice, uniting divine and human consciousness in profound healing. Through one-on-one Akashic Record sessions, research, and future-driven business consulting, she helps clients and visionaries uncover their soul's wisdom and embrace their fullest potential.

As the creator of the *Akashic Records Intensive*, the most comprehensive Akashic Records training, and author of *Akashic Records Masterclass*, Cheryl challenges the limits of what's possible in spiritual innovation. Her students and clients know her as relatable, insightful, and unafraid of the raw and real aspects of deep work.

When she's not writing, Cheryl is on the hiking trail, listening to nature's wisdom and exploring the heartbeat of the mountain.

Through her journey, she has distilled her intention for life to these seven words:

BELIEVE. Laugh. Learn. Love. Be. Become. Always.

CherylMarlene.com

AkashicRecordInsights.com

SpiritualDeepDive.com

ALSO BY CHERYL MARLENE

Akashic Records Masterclass

Masterclass includes these four books which may also be purchased separately:

What are the Akashic Records?

Open Your Akashic Records

Open the Akashic Records for Other

500 Questions to Ask the Akashic Records

The New Akashic Records

Akashic Records: Gemstone Guardians

Gemstone Guardians Journal

How to Navigate the Five Steps of Your Spiritual Journey

Soul Compass: Trusting Inner Truth to Navigate Life's Uncertainties

Soul Compass Companion Journal

---

www.ingramcontent.com/pod-product-compliance
Lightning Source LLC
LaVergne TN
LVHW051103080426
835508LV00019B/2038